THE LAVA NEVER SLEEPS
A HONOLULU MEMOIR

LOREEN LILYN LEE

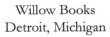

Willow Books
Detroit, Michigan

The Lava Never Sleeps: A Honolulu Memoir

Editor: Lisa Allen
Cover art: Aquarius Press
Author photo: Mel Ponder Photography

ISBN 978-1-7322091-5-2
LCCN 2019936101

Willow Books, a Division of Aquarius Press
www.WillowLit.net

Printed in the United States of America

To my mother Mildred Wong Lee (1918-1998)
whose love of books continues to fill my heart
and mind with worlds of possibilities.

What would happen if one woman told the truth about her life ?
The world would split open.

—Muriel Rukeyser

Contents

Prologue

PART 1: KEIKI (CHILD)

PART 2: WAHINE (WOMAN)

PART 3: KEIKI O KA 'ĀINA (CHILD OF THE LAND)

Acknowledgments

Author's Note: Hawaiian words in the manuscript are punctuated according to Hawaiian language dictionaries and purposely not italicized. My intention is to avoid reinforcing Hawaiian culture as something exotic and/or foreign. Italics are applied for emphasis, titles, names of vessels, and direct quotes. Also, Hawaiian nouns have no plural forms; the same word is used for both singular and plural.

Some names and identifying details have been changed to protect the privacy of individuals.

Prologue

A pre-seminar crowd was buzzing with friendly chatter as I registered, got my name tag, then navigated my way into the ballroom. I looked attractive and confident. But my shoulder-length hair, permed into waves, my makeup, including false eyelashes, and my silk outfit disguised my true feelings: I felt disheveled and aimless, like a homeless bag lady.

The chairs in this Waikīkī hotel ballroom were arranged theater-style, perhaps two hundred or more, facing a platform where the two seminar leaders held our attention. They were thirty-something, vibrant, and charismatic. His premature silver-white, trimmed mane contrasted with her reddish auburn curls, reminding me of ice and fire. This husband and wife team, leaders of a small spiritual community on the island, conducted exercises instructing us to close our eyes and breathe deeply, "Relax and connect to a memory...." At the end of one of these exercises, they invited people to share. Several people raised their hands and spoke.

I raised my hand. When I stood, I suddenly reached for the chair in front of me and clutched it. Hard. I heard a piercing cry fill the room. I looked around. It was coming from me. From someplace deep inside that I didn't know existed.

The sound of old pain and anger erupted from my body—an uncontrollable primal scream.

Part 1: Keiki
(Child)

Chapter 1:
I'm Not Supposed to Tell

Family is supposed to be our safe haven. Very often, it's the place where we find the deepest heartache.
—Iyanla Vanzant

See this photo. That's Daddy in his business suit. He always wears a suit and tie for work. He dresses in the style of the successful Chinatown businessman that he is. His store is Yuen Chong Company Ltd., a large store in Honolulu selling Chinese imports from food to furniture as well as American canned goods. With his hair brushed back from his smooth forehead and his rimless glasses resting firmly on his nose, he is well-groomed and in control. In this photo, he looks rather hefty, his extra weight declaring both prosperity and solid authority.

My pretty, slim mother stands next to him. She wears a lightweight, rayon Chinese dress or cheongsam. Her black hair is parted on the side with finger waves and soft curls in a style popular in the 1950s.

My three brothers, two sisters, and I stand in front of them. My brothers wear cowboy shirts. We girls are dressed in silk tops with cloth frog buttons and matching silk pajama pants. Artificial flowers adorn our hair, short and curled like Mommy's, thanks to the beauty parlor. Having so many children is more evidence of Daddy's prosperity.

We're at John Rogers Airport, about forty of us. Family and friends have brought lei, garlands of carnations, orchids, plumeria, roses, and other fragrant flowers, to wish Daddy farewell. Daddy has so many lei, they reach past his ears. He's leaving for a business trip to the mainland and will be flying on that Pan Am plane sitting on the tarmac, a few steps beyond the chain-link fence. The plane is as huge as an office building—an amazing sight.

Picture-perfect, we appear to be a happy, middle-class, Chinese American family. In post-war Honolulu, we live in one of the newer houses in the

11

neighborhood, on Vineyard Street, only minutes away from Chinatown. We have many modern conveniences: an all-electric kitchen, a vacuum cleaner, and Venetian blinds. Daddy drives a late-model Buick sedan with a big chrome grille. Mommy doesn't have to work outside the home and gets help with the cleaning and laundry a few times a week. We are healthy, other than normal childhood illnesses and sister Joleen's asthma. When we attend private schools, we will demonstrate our academic prowess.

I am the middle daughter and fifth child of B.C. and Mildred—the one in the photo looking away from the camera, distracted by something on my right. I'm four and a head taller than younger sister Joleen standing in front of me, staring at the camera while eating her Tootsie Roll lollipop. Older brothers Clyde and Ben are whispering and shoving each other. They're just being boys, so no one scolds them. After the photo is taken, our parents turn away from their crowd of children. They talk to our aunties and uncles. We scatter and join our cousins.

Going to the airport is always a special occasion since airplane travel is still a novelty in the mid-1950s. Hawaiian musicians wearing colorful aloha shirts and muʻumuʻu sing and play their instruments; hula dancers perform barefoot, telling stories with graceful hands; shops offer gifts from Hawaiʻi and fresh lei. Arrivals and departures attract throngs of relatives and friends ready with their good wishes and garlands, bought from one of the vendors or strung from flowers grown at home in their yards. The travelers are easy to identify in their suits and hats, as required in these early days of air travel.

When passengers climb the steps into the plane, they turn with a final wave before disappearing through the door. Propellers roar into action and become a blur. We cover our ears and close our eyes as the wind churned up by the propellers blows against us and raises dust. The plane takes off while we keep waving and waving until it turns into a shiny dot that disappears into the sky.

~~~

I was born in March 1949. In August of that same year, Mommy became pregnant again. Nine months later, April showers brought Joleen just after my first birthday. I still needed my mother: her attention and her touch, her devotion and closeness. Who was this crying interloper anyway? The spotlight now shone on Joleen, and I didn't like it, not one bit. It was bad enough that baby sister was so darn cute. In addition, she had asthma, which required my parents' constant attention.

My mother loved children. However, I cannot imagine that another baby so soon could have been planned. She must have been exhausted with the physical and hormonal changes and certainly could not focus on me as much as she or I would have liked. When Joleen was born, I lost the coveted role as youngest.

In 2009, I was helping a friend with her infant and read some of her books about the care and development of infants. I felt a twinge of recognition of what I had lost. Current parenting books advise parents to reassure babies so they feel secure in their world. In the early months, parents should respond to their babies' crying. Neglecting me may not have been intentional, but Mommy had no one to help her. By August, I was only six months old. Not only was Mommy pregnant, but she had four other young children to care for. Her sisters-in-law were not supportive. Besides, they were raising their own families. It would not have been appropriate for her to ask for help outside of the Lee clan. Daddy was working and relied on Mommy to manage the house and children. There was no one for her.

~~~

Before her marriage, friends had warned her: "Watch out for B.C.'s sisters. They can be mean." However, Mommy could not have foreseen such hostility from her sisters-in-law when she moved into the household with Daddy's mother and three unmarried siblings: Auntie Mag, Auntie Ninny, and Uncle Sonny. While Auntie Betty and Auntie Jo were married and lived in their own houses, they often visited. (I didn't know about Auntie Katie, their beloved oldest sister until many years later; her unexpected death in the 1930s had so wounded the family that she was never mentioned.)

The aunties criticized her: "What do you mean you don't know how to cook? Can't you cook anything? Not even rice? A grown woman… unbelievable! Can you bake? Can you sew? Crochet? You don't know much, do you?!"

It was true. Mommy could not cook as a young woman. Her parents had spoiled her and didn't allow her to cook even when she was old enough and capable, so she entered into marriage with a deficit. She had to take cooking classes downtown at Hawaiian Electric Company, while Daddy taught her some basic Chinese dishes. Although the aunties laughed at her lack of domestic skills—areas they excelled in, they could not fault her for not producing children. Between 1943 and 1950, she gave her husband six children. And with her delicate features and trim waist, she remained pretty and stylish between pregnancies, whether in pleated trousers and blouse or rayon dresses with padded shoulders.

Those sisters-in-law, who had borne sons, now wanted daughters. Mommy had the audacity to produce a daughter before any of them. She had no control over this, of course, but her timing must have inflamed their rancor.

They never missed an opportunity to criticize her. "You made these noodles? Too salty." I wasn't supposed to hear the little knives come out when they spoke to her. We children were extensions of her and easy targets. I had to pretend to not notice the lavish presents they gave our cousins while we received underwear. I had to ignore how their voices sharpened when they spoke to me compared to more gentle tones with others.

~~~

When I hear stories about someone's father giving them money when they ask for it, they sound like fairy tales to me. My siblings and I dreaded asking Daddy for money. Simply hated it. Daddy made us cower as he breathed fire, rumbling and grumbling around the house. Daddy would rail at Mommy, "What happened to the money I gave you at the beginning of the month? You should have enough for the kids! Did you spend it all? How can it all be gone already?"

We always asked Mommy first and prayed she'd have what we needed for our bus fares or school lunches or some school fees. If not, we'd have to ask Daddy. He'd finally give us the money, but the feelings of humiliation and diminishment stuck to the money. With eyes cast down, we slunk quietly away. Our hair, clothes, and souls singed.

I don't know how much she got every month, if it was enough, or if she did indeed mismanage her spending. If I had to guess, I would bet her allowance had not increased as we grew from children into teens, reflecting our growing needs and costs. And so, we all suffered Daddy's tirades when we made a simple request: "Can I have fifty cents for lunch?" Sometimes to avoid a confrontation, Mommy would sneak into Daddy's wallet and take what was needed. It felt like a death-defying act, both frightening and thrilling to witness. It was like watching her sneak into the dragon's den to get the treasure while the dragon was sleeping. But we did not fault her. We also would have resorted to covert operations to escape his verbal abuse.

At the time, I never questioned that Mommy didn't have her own money. As an adult, she should not have had to ask someone else for money. She had worked as a bookkeeper in Daddy's store before they married and was not an irresponsible person. Instead of giving her expense funds once a month, Daddy could have given her allotments twice a month. Or he could have simply given her more cash. There were other options. Instead, he was stubborn, controlling, set in his ways, and certainly did not invite discussion from my mother for remedying the situation.

~~~

We never talked about conflicts in the family—not conflicts with relatives, not conflicts among ourselves. They were simply ignored, wished away. Similarly, any tensions between cultures in the islands remained subterranean. Not everyone wanted statehood. In the 1950s and decades prior, controversy still raged in some quarters about annexation and how haole (white) business interests had stolen the Kingdom of Hawai'i and overthrown her queen.

When I was born here in the middle of the twentieth century, Hawai'i was not yet a state. With the Philippines, Puerto Rico, and Guam, Hawai'i became annexed in 1898 as United States territories after the Spanish-American War. It was a time of American expansionism, and Hawai'i had proven valuable as a supply station for U.S. battleships en route to the Philippines.

Business interests in Hawai'i, led by prosperous descendants of missionaries, had long petitioned the United States to annex these islands to gain favorable terms for Hawai'i's sugar industry, but the 1897 treaty of annexation failed to pass with the required two-thirds votes. Petitions with tens of thousands of signatures, mostly those of native Hawaiians, flooded the halls of Congress objecting to annexation. However, mounting pressure by business and military interests spurred the House of Representatives to circumvent normal channels by introducing a joint resolution, which needed only a simple majority to pass. When President McKinley signed the resolution in 1898, hope fizzled for those who opposed annexation and for Queen Lili'uokalani, who hoped to reclaim her kingdom and her sovereignty.

As territorial residents, we were American citizens. Our address was Honolulu, T.H. (Territory of Hawai'i).

Whether out in the open or not, this environment of conflict became my world. Mommy didn't complain; she never spoke negatively about my aunties or anybody, at least not that I ever heard. Daddy was the family patriarch and he had chosen her; when she asked him to intervene and speak to his sisters, he failed to defend her. While they could be a royal pain with their resentment and sniping, no matter what, she was still B.C.'s wife. She would rise above their petty ways, their disrespect, and hold her ground. By traditional Chinese standards, as the wife of the eldest son, she "outranked" her sisters-in-law. She knew they were just waiting for her to show a sign of weakness. She would not give them this satisfaction; she would rather die than ask any of them for help.

I was only a child, but I felt the tension. I was not supposed to feel scared in my bones, so conscious of my every breath, my every step as if the Big Bad Wolf with big sharp teeth was waiting to devour me.

~~~

Auntie Mae stands out from my other aunties. Not only is she the tallest woman I've ever seen, she likes being with us younger kids as much as with the adults. Her wide smile radiates over me and seems to animate the delicate flowers on her dress, its full skirt swaying as she walks. When she sees me, she crouches down and says, "Is this little Loreen?" and hugs me. She must have read my mind because suddenly I am firmly in her arms, above the others. I hold on as my face brushes against the loose, graying curls that frame her face. I smell the carnation lei she was wearing earlier and lean into her welcoming body. She sits down and holds me in her lap.

After this introduction, I look forward to seeing this auntie from California, that wondrous, faraway place that I imagine is populated with sweet, happy, tall people. We call all adults "auntie" and "uncle" in the islands, and it doesn't matter to me that she is not a real auntie. Our families are bonded by friendship and business. Auntie Mae is real to me. I lift my arms to her whenever I see her. Without hesitation, she responds with open arms. I can be my five-year-old self when I am with her, without wariness. I can breathe and relax. I like the pretty dresses she wears, and they don't wrinkle when I sit on her lap. I've known kindness from adults, but physical affection is not common between adults nor between adults and children in my family.

Auntie Mae doesn't appear old or fragile although she is older than my parents and other aunties. One day as I am sitting in her lap, one of my younger aunties comes over. She looks at me and says, "Shame on you! You're too old to be carried." Her words bite into my skin. The pleasure of human contact dissipates while the heat of shame fills my body. I clamber down from her lap. Auntie Mae tries to protest, "No. It's all right…" But I dare not disobey. I understand adults have power and authority, but voices tinged with anger or irritation trump others. I learn quickly—wanting to be near Auntie Mae can mean trouble from others. But she soon returns to her home across the ocean, and that's that.

~~~

I discern the dividing line between children and adults. Adults are clearly in charge. I learn the rules: where to be, where not to be, how to behave. I'm not supposed to understand adult things. If I do, I'm not supposed to tell.

I'm not supposed to tell when adults are mean or unfair to me or others…when I see or hear things I'm not supposed to see or hear…when someone gives me a present I don't like. I'm not supposed to tell stories about the family that are embarrassing or can reflect negatively.

Don't talk.

Don't tell.

Don't talk back.

Be quiet.

But I can't help myself. I cannot stop what I see and hear. I cannot stop my secret voice from talking to me.

Chapter 2:
Honolulu Sweet and Sour

Pain engraves a deeper memory.
—Anne Sexton

Candy bars, Life Savers, Tootsie Rolls, Violets, Cracker Jacks, Necco Wafers, Jujubes, nonpareils, wax bottles filled with sweet liquids, chewing gum, and bubble-gum jawbreakers. You name it—we wanted it and we ate it all. My five siblings and I had many options for that feel-good sugar.

We always had candy in the house. Family friends often brought back boxes of See's candies from their mainland trips. Christmas brought a bonanza: jars of hard candies, Whitman's Sampler boxes of chocolates, pink tins of Almond Roca, and boxes of Frango Mints. We devoured all of it though it took us a few months; there was such bounty. However, the neighborhood grocery store was our regular supplier. There Mommy would let each of us choose a sweet treat.

My favorite was Botan Rice Candy from Japan—the magical chewy candy wrapped in bits of colored wax paper. After unwrapping a piece, another clear "wrapper" surrounded the candy. I put it in my mouth and the wrapper melted away. On one end of the colorful box a small green compartment contained a surprise toy. This was the candy that kept on giving: I got candy and a toy for the same money.

We even had candy lei that we wore like necklaces. At the airport, we greeted adults with traditional flower lei. Brilliant shades of red, purple, fuchsia, yellow, orange, pink plus the fragrances of island flowers—plumeria, orchid, rose, carnation, tuberose, pīkake (jasmine)—offered a sensory experience of aloha. However, we children preferred wearing our garlands of cellophane-wrapped candies and packs of chewing gum tied together with ribbons, which promised sweet enjoyment later.

~~~

In a time when corporal punishment went unquestioned, Daddy beat his children with wire hangers and rubber slippers. He wanted it known throughout the land: He would toughen up his boys and take no back talk, no excuses. His children would not grow up to be lazy good-for-nothings. By the time we numbered six, he expected the elder sons, Clyde and Ben, to set an example for us younger siblings: Study hard, get good grades, do chores without having to be told. His loud scolding meant they had not measured up. Slaps on the head and threats—"Do I need to get the stick to get you moving?"—made me stop whatever I was doing. I froze, stopped breathing. What had they done that was so bad? Even though I was safe from his wrath, being the fifth child, I cowered anyway making my six-year-old body as small as possible.

~~~

Chilled Jell-O or Japanese kanten—I loved cold treats! American gelatin desserts were soft and wiggly, colored like jewels and fruit flavored. Japanese ones could be sliced into squares, picked up and eaten by hand; usually red or green, they were peppermint-flavored.

Ice cream—every type was yummy: sandwiches, drumsticks, Creamsicles, popsicles, ice cream bonbons. I stood in front of the little freezer at the neighborhood grocery store and peered in. What did I want today? Something on a stick or in a cup? What flavor? The bonbons we got at the movie theater were special treats: bite-size vanilla ice cream covered with chocolate—a little crunch and then cold creaminess.

We devoured all kinds of tropical fruits, chilled or not: juicy mangoes, papayas, lichee, star fruits, pineapple, apple bananas. Smaller than the common banana in grocery stores, the local apple bananas were sweet and tangy.

And sugarcane—I enjoyed chewing on sticks of sugar cane. My uncle cut a stalk from the sugarcane plant in our yard, peeled back the tough outer bark to get to the sweet core, which he sliced into sticks we could chew on. It was sweet, but not too sweet. My teeth had to grind the fibrous cane to extract the juice, then I'd spit out the pulp. It was more work than eating a piece of candy, for sure. Yet there was something satisfying in working for that taste.

~~~

Some days, as soon as Daddy set foot in the door, he began railing at

Mommy in Cantonese. If we had had a dog, he would have kicked it. If we were playing on the floor, the volume and tone of his voice warned us to get out of his way. Mommy took the verbal blows silently. She stood with eyes lowered and shoulders slumped and waited until Daddy was done. My throat tightened and hurt. He then shifted his anger to my brothers.

"What's the matter with you?! I work hard all day. Do I need to come home and do *your* work too? Who was mowing the grass? Why isn't it done? *Gunfunnit!!*" His roars made him more ominous as he stormed through the house, his face flushed with rage.

Maybe they had not finished the yard work, left out the lawnmower, or forgotten to take out the garbage. When he brought his rotten day home from work, a big black cloud accompanied him, so it didn't matter what they had done or not done.

Clyde and Ben, thirteen and eleven, brushed tears from their eyes. They darted past me and out the door to finish whatever needed to be done. My big brothers reduced to tears or trying to hide their tears cracked something inside me. Even though they existed in a different sphere from me, I still felt loyal to them. I knew fear and pain. And I knew it was us against them: kids against the adults. Size mattered. It represented power.

~~~

Shave ice was a favorite treat during my childhood. We bought shave ice in a paper cone in a rainbow of flavors: lime-green, purple-grape, strawberry-red, pineapple-yellow, and orange-orange. Banana-flavored syrup was a startling turquoise blue. At the store, the man or woman got a small block of ice from the ice cream freezer and placed it in their machine. They activated the machine with a foot pedal while holding the paper cone under the ice to catch the fine ice crystals, which they mounded into a huge dome that appeared as big as my head. After adding the syrups, they handed the cone to me. I received it carefully with both hands, not sure if I could finish it all by myself. Finely shaved ice that melted in my mouth was best, not the crunchy kind I had to chew—mm-mm, cold and sweet. I felt the cold entering my body, cooling it against the sticky heat of the day. Within fifteen minutes, I was drinking the last melted bits through a straw and smiled with satisfaction, unaware of my stained lips and mouth.

Malolo brand syrup, a local product, was a staple in our home. Simply add water to a little syrup to concoct the desired sweetness. We mixed orange, strawberry, or fruit punch syrups with water and ice in a pitcher to quench our thirst. We were always thirsty. Sometimes we poured the mixture into small paper cups or ice cube trays to make ice cakes.

~~~

Solidarity among the six of us children became impossible when the girls were pitted against the boys. While we were evenly matched in numbers—three girls and three boys—before 1959 when another son was born, we girls didn't stand a chance. My father's preferential treatment of his sons occurred throughout my life. If we had steak for dinner, the boys got the larger or better pieces. If my brother and I worked in Daddy's store, he would get paid and I wouldn't. If there wasn't enough dessert for everyone, the boys would definitely get served first. Later on in life, I learned that my sisters Marleen and Joleen worked throughout college because they paid for their own tuition, while Dad supported my brothers' college expenses. I remained ignorant of this inequity because I had received some scholarship money, then dropped out of college.

My father's predisposition toward his sons over his daughters impacted me from the time I was a young child. These vignettes represent a fraction of many unconscious acts that conveyed a clear message that we daughters were inferior.

Look and See

See the little girl run and play. See her read books. See her look at
her father and be ready to go with him on his Sunday drives.
Her father says, "Come on, son. Let's go for a drive."
*
See the little girl go to school. See her study. She is happy in school.
She has friends. Her teachers like her. She is smart and her report cards show this.
Her father says, "Look at my sons. They are scholars! How proud I am of my sons."
*
See the little girl be a good daughter. She is quiet and obedient.
She is helpful without needing to be asked. She helps her mother with the laundry.
She helps her father in his Chinatown store, just like her brother.
Her father says, "Look at my son. He is such a good boy!
Here's a dollar for working so hard."
*
See the little girl smile. Her mouth looks happy. But her eyes have no light.

21

Dad's relentless favoritism stemmed from Confucian values: Sons carry on the family name while daughters do not. Thus, girls are deemed superfluous. They marry out, take another family's name, and are absorbed into other families. Like putty, the fate of women lies in the hands of their fathers, brothers, husbands, sons. This patriarchal system values women's ability to bear children only when they produce males.

~~~

Temples of pastries and desserts—we visited them frequently. Walking into a bakery, I got giddy with anticipation. My nose was immediately taken prisoner with the aroma of freshly baked goods, my eyes glazing over when I stood before the shiny glass cases filled with pies, cakes, cookies, donuts.

Liliha Bakery produced our birthday cakes—banana sheet cakes decorated with roses of buttercream frosting—and other favorites: custard pies, lemon meringue pies, cream puffs, chocolate éclairs. Leonard's Bakery was famous for its loaves of Portuguese sweet bread, an island favorite sweetened with honey, and for malasadas, a chewy-textured donut puff sprinkled with sugar.

Some cakes and pies, like macadamia-nut cream and banana cream, required refrigeration with their mounds of whipped cream. We headed to Dee Lite Bakery for these fine desserts. Visions of guava chiffon cakes, haupia (coconut pudding) cakes, liliko'i (passion fruit) chiffon cakes, and dream cakes still dance in my head. Eating dream cake was like eating sweet clouds: multiple layers of light chocolate cake swathed with whipped cream in between, on top, and around the sides, sprinkled with curls of shaved chocolate.

~~~

I could do nothing to please my father, to convince him I was as worthy as my brothers. Being dutiful and obedient as much as possible, I washed dishes, vacuumed, dusted, and helped when asked. I was an excellent student and received awards and honors in high school. I immersed myself in extracurricular activities, becoming news editor on the school newspaper, competing in the debate club, and participating in student council projects. None of this mattered. I didn't know if he knew or noticed. He said nothing. His face and body registered no emotion. I felt my sense of self being assaulted again and again for being a girl. Any bits of self-esteem became twisted; I believed I was unworthy and unlovable. Being invisible to him reinforced my feelings that I was insignificant and didn't deserve love.

In senior year at St. Andrew's Priory, I received the Junior Miss scholarship award. The judges selected me for academic excellence from all the public and private school contestants in the state. Both thrilled and surprised, my mother and I arrived home, me still dressed in my fuchsia gown. As we entered the living room, she quietly told Dad, "Loreen won the scholarship award tonight." I knew she was proud of me and hoped he might say something to acknowledge this achievement. He didn't look at me. He might have said, "Hmm." I went to my bedroom to undress and get ready for bed. This was one more rejection, one more hurtful quiet crime. One word would have been enough. Great! Or Congratulations! Anything would have been better than silence. Not being acknowledged rendered me invisible, left me feeling I had no value.

Stories about parents in China drowning, abandoning, or selling female children reinforced my worthless status. I didn't have to go far for such stories. My mother's impoverished birth mother also had been given away, or likely sold, by her family in Guangdong, China, into an unknown future across the ocean. Grandmother, or Po Po Wong, survived the long ocean voyage and arrived alone in Honolulu as a fifteen-year-old girl, a servant for a prosperous Chinese family. They married her off to a much older man, my grandfather or Gung Gung Wong. She had no choice. Others made these important decisions for her. After all, she was only a girl. Fortunately for Po Po Wong, both her employer and her husband had good hearts, for not all such stories ended well.

When I was in junior high, Mom explained why she had so many siblings. "When I was born, my parents were very poor and already had four children. They could not support another child, so they gave me to another Chinese couple to raise." This was in 1918. I believe, if she had been a boy, her father would have acted differently. In her birth family, she had two sisters and two brothers. In her adoptive family, she had two brothers; all three had been adopted and were well-loved. She said, "That's why you have so many aunties and uncles and cousins!"

(Since both sets of parents belonged to the Wong clan, Gung Gung Wong and Po Po Wong will refer to my mother's biological parents while Grandfather/Grandmother Wong will refer to her adoptive parents.)

I'm not sure which of these options for girls—death, abandonment, or denigration—is the cruelest. Generations of Chinese females have suffered such abuse.

~~~

Sweet potato tempura—this was a favorite from the okazuyas, the little mom 'n pop Japanese delis. Biting into the crunchy, golden, deep-fried batter and tasting the soft sweetness of the cooked potato gave me such pleasure that simply seeing them displayed activated my salivary glands. Sushi rice had another kind of sweetness—one not related to desserts of any kind. Mochi combined both taste and texture that delighted my mouth—round pink or white patties of smooth pounded rice, chewy rice dough dusted with rice flour on the outside around a center of sweet red-bean paste. Always a good snack or after-meal treat.

Japanese sweets were more tantalizing than Chinese ones. Steamed buns with sweet black beans or red beans, moon cakes, or crystallized fruits and vegetables were often available, rendering them less exciting to my palate. The exceptions that appealed to me were little egg tarts, or custard tarts, and deep-fried sesame balls, crunchy with a sweet red-bean paste or sweet shredded coconut in the center.

Crackseed and other preserved fruit we called mui were readily available in Daddy's Chinatown store. Mostly sweet and sticky, plum, cherry, apricot, mango, kumquat, ginger, lemon peel—all were wildly popular. Each piece was a whole small fruit, with seed or seedless. Some items like mango and ginger were shredded. Dry and salty varieties were available. And salty-sweet. For example, plums could be bought in various flavors: sweet and sticky, dried and salty, or dried and salty-sweet. In crackseed the seed of the fruit is cracked and mixed with the pulp. The fun of eating it was that you had to spit out the bits of seed—not that kids need any excuse for spitting.

~~~

Mom taught me this: When life turns bitter or sour, eat a piece of candy. Maybe sugar didn't really make me happy, but it did give me a rush. It activated my endorphins and helped me push aside painful moments, incomprehensible behavior, and abuse—at least temporarily. It couldn't resolve the pain or the problem, but it offered respite, a reprieve from life's hard edges.

I could swim away in the frothiness of my ice cream float or shrink my body to fit into the ring of a Life Savers® candy or float away on a sea of 7-Up®. I could pretend to be as light as a bubble-gum balloon and fly wherever the wind gusted or surrender to the coldness of a Creamsicle as anxiety and fear melted away for a little while. My mind could stop—please STOP!—thinking and wondering about things I had no power to change.

I craved the sweet innocence of childhood, unaware of Mom's hunger to soothe *her* body, mind, and heart.

Chapter 3:
Family Life and Lessons

It's the questions we can't answer that teach
us the most. They teach us how to think.
—Patrick Rothfuss

ok! Pok! Pok! Rain tapped on the large, paddle-shaped leaves of ti plants and heliconia outside the bedroom window. This music of the rain soothed me. I drifted off to sleep. Sometimes a fast drip: pokpokpokpokpokpok. Sometimes slow: pok... pok... pok... pok. Tropical storms blew in leaden skies full of dark heavy clouds, the drama of thunder and lightning, and torrents of rain, sometimes aslant on blustery days. When the streets flooded, schools canceled classes and children cheered.

A storm brought exciting dark clouds to our normally sunny skies. Still, I anticipated bright, sunny days one after another, feeling the warm sun upon my burnished skin. A drizzle sometimes dampened hair and clothes, while the sun continued blazing against a blue sky—refusing to hide its glory behind the interloping clouds. This "liquid sunshine" came and went quickly, watering both people and plants, and left the air and earth cool and freshened. Arcs of colors splashed across the sky, filling me with wonder.

~~~

Mommy dressed me every morning in neatly pressed cotton dresses, buttoning up the back of the dress and tying back my sash into a crisp bow. She combed my short, straight black hair and bangs. My older siblings had left for their respective schools, so with me on one hand and Joleen on the other, Mommy walked me to kindergarten along our tree-lined street: up our short asphalt driveway, turning right for a few yards to a crosswalk. We looked right and left before stepping into the two-lane street and continued straight ahead into the schoolyard, which sloped gently down from the sidewalk.

The school building, clean and modest, stood amidst large monkey pod trees that shaded the playground. My eyes flew to the swings, see-saws, sliding boards, a sandbox, a jungle gym. On weekends, the teachers locked up the tall chain-link gate, which didn't stop us. We kids found ways to sneak in. Most of us were small enough to carefully squeeze through the narrow opening between gate and gatepost. The bigger kids found a low spot under the chain-link fence, made it deeper by digging out more dirt, and slithered their bodies under the fence. I ran over to the swings and kicked my feet into the dirt, already scooped out by the feet of many other children, then pumped my knees back and forth to push the swing higher and higher. It felt like flying as I stretched out my toes toward the leaves at the tips of the branches in the tall monkey pod tree. If I dared to let go of the swing, I imagined drifting off into the sky above the playground like a balloon.

~~~

I loved playing pretend. Joleen and I played house with our dolls; we "mommies" took care of our "babies" and put them in a carriage to go shopping. We played fashion show with Mommy's old purses and shoes; for long hair, we fastened scarves to our heads with bobby pins and let them flow down our backs. We pretended sophistication with candy cigarettes; we drew in our breath sucking on the end of any candy stick, and blew out the "smoke" while holding the candy between the index and middle finger, as we'd seen on television.

One day in school, Mrs. So, our principal, asked if anyone could dance or sing. The school was planning an open-house program for parents and wanted to showcase the talents of the children. My hand shot up and I announced, "I can dance ballet." The words tumbled out before I could stop myself. I had watched my big sister in ballet class and positively knew if I wore her tutu, I would transform into a ballerina. Three years older, my sister was at a suitable age to follow formal instruction for specific movements. Watching her in class, I didn't understand the precision required and the need for practice and control. Whatever she was doing, I wanted to do too.

The night of the performance arrived, and Mommy was helping me in the dressing room. A frenzy of excitement took hold of me; I was anxious to wear sister's ballet costume, which I'd frequently peeked at hanging in the closet. Now Mommy was helping me into the pink tights, then I was stepping into the pink tutu. The silky feeling of the shiny satin bodice against my skin and the way the stiff skirt extended out in a little circle, layers of netting fabric right below the waist, gave me tingles. The ballet slippers were black with a little elastic band across each foot. I stood there ready.

Suddenly the light turned on in the little playhouse of my mind. Inside I felt like I had swallowed rocks—big rocks. Looking up, I whispered, "Mommy, I don't know how to dance. What should I do?" This wasn't a magic tutu after all, so I was in big trouble. She remained calm, quietly combed my hair and applied lipstick to my mouth, some rouge to my cheeks. I had to figure out something quickly.

I had of course mimicked the movements that big sister did in her classes numerous times, playing as if I knew what I was doing. The movements looked easy enough. Hold your arms up like this. Jump. Put your feet like this, now bend, now straighten. After volunteering, I gave no thought to the performance, didn't think I should practice. I believed in the magical tutu. In the next few minutes I would find out if playing and actually performing were the same.

I heard Mrs. So announce my name. I stepped out of the dressing room and stood facing the audience. My classmates and their parents sat on folding wooden chairs, their faces friendly and expectant. No turning back now. The music on the record player began. Except for this, silence surrounded me— me in a borrowed tutu. The room seemed to expand. Instead of a cozy room full of friendly people, everyone became hazy like a mirage, shrinking in the distance. Their eyes grew large and fastened on me.

My mind filled with sparkly light. I blinked and saw the faces of the beautiful ballerinas in my favorite coloring book. In the next instant, two of them appeared beside me in the kindergarten classroom, one on either side. They were much taller than I had imagined, or maybe the shiny sequins on their costumes were distorting my vision. We began to dance. Together. Following their leaps and twirls, suddenly I was aware of a warm glow filling my body that dissolved the heavy rocks I'd felt before. This inner light infused me with warmth, like drinking hot cocoa and feeling a sweet, sweet certainty that all will be well. When the music stopped, I bowed and the audience clapped and clapped. When I looked up, the ballerinas were gone. I was alone again, but without that heavy, sinking feeling.

Mrs. So had been pleased when I volunteered that I was certain she had discussed it with my mother, who walked me to and from school every day. "We're so delighted that Loreen will be dancing for our program!" What could

Mommy have said that would not expose me as a liar or reflect unfavorably on her as a parent? She never discussed this incident with me, either before or after. Not one word. Never chided me. Never offered any words of comfort or encouragement when I panicked right before the performance. No words of relief when I didn't stumble, fall, or make a fool of myself.

No questions. No comments. Nothing unusual. By some miracle, my performance went well; a potential tropical storm had turned into sunshine. Perhaps there really was nothing to talk about. Perhaps she had faith in me and my abilities. Or perhaps Mommy knew that a five-year-old in a tutu can do no wrong.

The silence between adults and children remained intact. But the door into another realm, a different quality of silence, serene and without contention, was now open to me.

~~~

As a man from China, my father embraced the strictures and age-old traditions espousing the omnipotence of parental authority, the unquestioning obedience of children, and a "universal wisdom" that created males superior to females. He had learned well from his father (my grandfather or Gung Gung) and was ready to step into the role of family patriarch when Gung Gung Lee died in 1935. Raised in the nineteenth century, Gung Gung Lee characterized parental strictness, and Dad followed suit in raising us, his twentieth-century family. Dad didn't know how to talk to his children. However, no discussion was necessary since he made all the decisions. He didn't have to understand us or know how we felt.

Dad was comfortable being in control, managing people. He was the general manager for Yuen Chong Company, a large, well-known Chinese import store in Honolulu's Chinatown located at 83 North King Street between Maunakea and Bethel Streets.

His office, on the mezzanine where he could survey the sales floor and the old nickel-plated cash register, was furnished with an old-fashioned roll-top desk, a black metal safe against the wall, and a large table-top desk facing the room. From this outpost, he worked or read the newspaper while observing the bookkeepers at their desks nearby and the bustling activity in the store below, both customers and salesclerks. He could hear the deliveryman talking with customers on the phone or directing the warehouse workers in the back of the building. When friends and business associates dropped by, we could hear their approach as they clanked up the metal stairs to his office or else he went downstairs to greet them.

With a big smile, Daddy extended his arm to shake someone's hand with a firm grip. "Hi, long time no see. Come, have a seat." Daddy could be all-business, but he also had his jovial side. I marveled at how talkative he became with non-family members, switching back and forth between English and Cantonese as needed.

Because the store was Daddy's world, it became our world too. While my older siblings attended school, Mommy took me and my younger sister on outings. After dressing herself and applying her makeup, she helped us into our dresses and Mary Jane shoes to ride the bus to Chinatown. We visited open markets for fresh vegetables and fish or Chinese roast pork. Many older Chinese women dressed in long, loose Chinese dresses, with their hair pulled back into buns at the nape of their necks, also shopped in Chinatown. Inevitably, one or two would stop to say hello to my mother. She and Daddy were well-known in the Chinese community. After lunch at one of the restaurants, we arrived at Daddy's store.

As we approached the store, we saw the two huge display windows on either side of large double doors that stayed open six days a week. The doors were wood paneled—teak with glass windows. And the display windows were large enough for an adult to climb into to arrange the merchandise in an attractive way. Chinese lanterns hung above boxes of firecrackers, boxes of dried noodles, various Chinese dishes, and cooking utensils for woks. Upon entering the store, the smoke and noxious smell of a cigar assaulted me. I pinched my nose and quickly walked past. The man who worked behind the liquor counter, where cigars and cigarettes were also sold, puffed on a cigar, oblivious to anyone's discomfort. This section was only for adults. Near the doors, excelsior and Chinese newspaper strips spilled out of crates and barrels onto the dull linoleum floor and revealed Chinese hand-painted bowls nested inside.

Some crates held two kinds of preserved eggs—a Chinese delicacy known as hundred-year-old or thousand-year-old eggs. Duck eggs, packed in black clay for several months, become transformed: The yolks turn a grayish green and the whites solidify and become brownish and translucent. Mommy often served these eggs as side dishes for Daddy, so we got to see and taste them. They were very popular among local people, not only Chinese customers.

Inside the store, I headed to the back where a refrigerated case held bottles of soda pop. Past the shelves of American canned goods against one wall, the glass cabinets on the other side of the store displayed gift items with Chinese cookbooks on top; a large counter occupied the middle of the store with cubbyholes for various sizes of brown paper bags, wrapping paper, spindles of string and ribbon; an old cash register anchored this counter on the far end. I reached into the cold air among the soda bottles and looked for an orange soda. With sodas in hand, Mommy, my sister, and I climbed the stairs up to Daddy's office. I knew his job was important even though I didn't understand what he did.

We heard stories that the store was founded in 1885. When Gung Gung Lee arrived in Honolulu in 1887, he became an employee and later, a partner. Hawai'i was still a monarchy at the time, with King David Kalākaua on the throne. The political landscape was murky. The descendants of white missionaries, having accrued power and wealth, became cabinet members and forced the king to sign a new constitution, described (for good reason) as the "Bayonet Constitution." The lives of most immigrants centered on daily survival—food, home, and work. And since many could not read or write in any language, local politics would not have been of primary interest.

I don't know where or how Gung Gung Lee accumulated the money to invest in the store and become a merchant. He was only fifteen when he immigrated from his village in Guangdong, China, where most of Honolulu's Chinese originated. He did not speak English or Hawaiian. He connected with his fellow countrymen, who spoke the same dialect and offered advice in finding a job and a place to live. He blended into his new-found community wearing his native clothing and long braid down his back. He started out as a cook, I think. The back of the store had an old kitchen, as it was common for Chinese stores to provide meals for their all-male employees.

Chinatown was a haven for new immigrants like my grandfather. Stores, restaurants, and other businesses flourished with the influx of Chinese laborers for the plantations. The stores became community centers where these immigrants could socialize and purchase items. They also acted as "post offices" for letters to and from China.

Gung Gung Lee was fortunate; he didn't have to take one of those back-breaking plantation jobs in the hot Hawaiian sun. I can only imagine that he was ambitious and savvy enough to make the most of his opportunities in this new land, eventually becoming store manager and prosperous enough to bring his wife and son from China. At some point, he cut off his queue and adapted a more Western appearance: short hair and business suits. When Dad inherited this position, he expanded upon his father's reputation by joining the board of directors at Liberty Bank, which was located next to the store and run by Chinese businessmen. Like his father, he exhibited his prominence in the community by wearing a suit and tie.

~~~

Mom helped in the store occasionally, especially during the holidays. As a former employee, she was familiar with the store. That's how she and Dad met. As her husband, Dad was still her boss.

One of the busiest times was Chinese New Year. The Chinese community purchased ingredients for special holiday dishes, firecrackers, and presents, while restaurants increased their orders to prepare for New Year dinner parties. Our entire family descended on the store to witness the community celebration and absorb all the good luck and excitement floating through Chinatown. At night, streets filled with people waiting for the many-legged lion amid a cacophony of firecrackers, gongs, and drums that accompanied the dancing lion, which stopped at each business. Both were essential for good luck in the Lunar New Year. All the activity excited and frightened me. The smoke from the firecrackers burned my throat and eyes. The lion was huge, flapping its large gaping mouth and directing its large eyes at me. I had to be carried to see above everyone's heads, but when the lion looked at me, I covered my eyes. Even though the black slacks of the teenage boys and girls, who brought this mythical creature to life, were visible, the wagging lion's head seemed enormous and all-too-real.

When my siblings and I got older, we were recruited to help with the annual inventory. January 1 was inventory day and all the employees and Lee children gathered in the store—the more people, the faster the work would be accomplished. Everything needed to be counted or weighed—each can, each dish, each bottle, each package of gum; gingko nuts, dried mushrooms, crackseed, watermelon seeds, pine nuts, red dates, dried shrimps, Chinese sausages, pressed duck, preserved eggs. We were reluctant workers, but Dad gave us no choice and we complied, fully knowing any whining or grumbling would do no good.

In fifth grade, I was allowed to walk to Chinatown after school to wait for Daddy and ride home with him. Sometimes I would find a spot to do some homework in his office. He was busy at his desk and the beads on his abacus clicked quickly as he calculated. Other times I helped out by stocking shelves, wrapping presents for customers, packaging dried mushrooms, dried scallops, or black fungus into cellophane bags, or helping customers find things. I was eager to get Daddy's attention and win his approval.

Without question, the locus of Daddy's power was the store, and I hovered there, enthralled with the possibility of his mere glance in my direction.

~~~

At family dinners in our home, kids knew to stay out of the way of adults. Cousins, siblings, and I went to play in the "courtyard," as we called this large room adjacent to the main house. It wasn't a true courtyard— usually an open-air space enclosed by four walls of a building. Instead, our house formed an L-shape with two additional walls constructed to form a rectangular room with a roof covered by sheets of fiberglass that filtered the sunlight. Grass mats softened the concrete-slab floor, while window screens at the top of the new walls welcomed the cooling trade winds.

Stepping into the courtyard from the house, we children had a number of choices: On our right was the door leading out to the yard, to swings suspended from a metal frame, to trees—mango, lichee, starfruit, fig—and the greenhouse where Uncle Clem, who lived next door, grew orchids; on the left, along the wall of the house ran a wide, dark green Formica countertop; and in front of us, an open space with built-in bookshelves along one side and the back wall. Beyond the counter was a small landing leading to a door into the house where two bedrooms were located. Stepping down from the landing, we came to an old bookshelf with glass windows along the wall. The books that attracted me and were within reach were the orange-covered Childcraft series.

The counter held multiple possibilities. A workspace for Daddy's household projects and repairs. A buffet area for party foods. A runway when we played dress-up in Mommy's old clothes, scarves, and handbags; we made our grand entrance from the usually locked door down the length of the counter then pivoted to turn around to walk back. A stage for hula performances by older sister Marleen and her friends, for make-believe performances and play-acting. And a jumping-off point for little boys eager to prove their fierceness as cowboys and Indians, yelling, "Geronimo!" as they leaped off mountain cliffs.

The courtyard functioned as party room and playground, where adults sent us to scream and carry on with little concern for noise. We played here during parties, on rainy days, or when it was too hot and humid outdoors. I have mostly fond memories of the courtyard, including when we became older and played card games or listened to our records on the hi-fi stereo there.

So, when our house swarmed with extended family, for example, at our Lee family dinners, we kids knew we belonged in the courtyard, where we played or read comic books—Superman, Batman, Archie, and Little Lulu. With the older kids made responsible for the younger ones, we numbered sixteen-plus children of various ages. The adults—at least twelve, more if close family friends were invited—took over the living and dining rooms, where they would talk-story while smoking Lucky Strikes and drinking highballs with lots of ice clinking in their tall glasses. Straight hair was old-fashioned so the women's hair had been styled and curled at the beauty salon or with a home permanent. They wore sleeveless cotton blouses with modified Mandarin collars and coconut shell buttons and slacks or pedal pushers, while the men wore aloha shirts with popular border prints.

My aunties and Mom flew back and forth into the kitchen to help prepare food, serve the men their drinks, and clean up. Except for Dad, the men stayed out of the kitchen. Dad was a good cook and took charge of roasting a leg of lamb, rib roast, chicken or turkey. When the meat was done, he removed the pan from the oven and let it sit, with the meat still sizzling, and later removed the roast from the pan to the large cutting board on the kitchen table. Mom would make gravy from the pan drippings, while Dad took pleasure in sharpening the carving knife. When I heard the knife blade scraping back and forth on the sharpening rod, I knew Dad was getting ready to carve. I took my place near the kitchen table to watch with an appreciative and expectant look, like a supplicant waiting for the communion bread and wine. He deftly sliced the meat and gave me a warm, juicy sample with its layer of crisp fat or crispy skin. This first morsel always tasted especially delicious coming from my father's hand, and I felt blessed.

With the table laden with food—Jell-O rescued from its molds, macaroni and tuna fish salad, chow mein noodles, olives and pickles, baked ham with pineapple, home-made rolls, carrot and raisin salad, roasted chicken, buns filled with Chinese pork, deep-fried won tons, and, of course, rice—the women helped the children with their plates, got them seated at one of the card tables set apart from the adults, then rejoined the men for their dinners.

We didn't use disposable plates much in the 1950s even for our buffet-style dinners, which occurred at least monthly. The aunties took care of cleaning up. When my sisters and I got older (I was about nine), we were expected to help. At first, it felt so grown-up to help my pretty aunties in the kitchen. However, I soon recognized it for the chore it really was—washing stacks of dishes produced ugly wrinkled fingers. Yet, good daughters learned to suffer in silence and to not question the absence of males (my brothers) during such chores.

We kids might also help serve dessert to the adults. Once, I approached some aunties and uncles sitting in a corner of the living room with a box of Whitman's candy. I did not sneak up on them. When I got close enough, I saw they were laughing and looking at a magazine, and I saw a picture of a naked woman.

I looked quickly away. "Would you like some candy?" They had not seen me approaching and swiftly closed the *Playboy* magazine. "What are you doing here? No, no. Go on, see if they want some over there." I was dismissed and left wondering, Why were they looking at naked women? Even though I had done nothing wrong, my face flushed with shame.

~~~

The sounds of daily life were many and varied: children yelling and playing, the discordant tones of Chinese opera music on the radio, the voices of neighbors speaking Japanese, Pidgin English, Cantonese, Korean, Filipino, the ringing of the telephone, sloshings of the washing machine, birds singing and chattering in the trees, cars swooshing by on the paved street. And yet, I was also keenly aware of vast silences, the lack of dialogue, what was not spoken.

My parents, or more precisely, my Dad defined the rules. Many were unspoken, yet unquestionably communicated by behavior. Don't talk back to adults. Don't ask questions; just do as you're told. Adults are always right. Being the middle girl, I didn't have a clearly-defined role in the family. Older sister became Mom's helper with cooking and cleaning, while baby sister's role was being cute with her soft, chubby cheeks; she could do no wrong. Sensing my own invisibility, I observed others and watched for opportunities to please the adults: ready to help out and offer compliments at a moment's notice. "That's a pretty sweater." Or "This pie is dee-licious."

I learned quickly. Silence was good, and noise was bad. Helping was good, and laziness, bad. Boys were good; girls, well, not so good. I could navigate through most of my days by analyzing good versus bad behavior and acted accordingly. However, this last item required a different strategy: I would have to prove I was as good and smart as my brothers. I didn't know how to accomplish this. It wasn't a conscious choice nor was it something open for discussion. Somehow, I had a strong sense of right and wrong, and this idea that boys were unquestionably good and girls questionable felt wrong. And unfair. I knew I had to do something to prove I was just as worthy. I knew this was a matter of personal survival.

~~~

My father decided what schools would provide the best education. We sisters attended a private all-girls school run by Episcopalian nuns, while our brothers went to Catholic schools. In addition to a Christian-based, college-prep environment, we observed all major Chinese holidays at home. And so, our minds became an unconscious blend of Christianity, Confucianism, and Taoism; at home we did as we were told by our parents; at school we did as we were told by the nuns and teachers. We were quiet and obedient at home, but at school we learned to speak up, ask questions, and participate in classroom discussions. I didn't question the need for dual personalities to accommodate my two environments nor did my parents and most other adults notice the juggling act required. Like a swarm of bees buzzing in my head, I wanted to know Why? Why? Why? Yet I knew better than to ask.

Questioning adults at home was impertinent and disrespectful—a punishable act. Curiosity and a desire for knowledge could easily die without encouragement; I followed the rules without allowing my good behavior to dull my mind and spirit. Indeed, I could not quell the questions bouncing around in my brain even though there was no possibility of expressing them.

~~~

Chinese holidays are occasions for taking care of and feeding the ancestors. In doing so, Chinese families honor them and ensure the ancestors will help the family, fulfilling the Confucian code of reciprocity. Actual food is prepared and set with chopsticks and drinks on a table, each item in its specific position in front of ancestral images like grandparents' portraits. The main feast days are the Lunar New Year, Ching Ming (Memorial Day) in April, the autumn Moon Festival, and Chinese Christmas (Winter Solstice).

On these feast days, Mom set up the card table in the living room and placed the tray with the red box of sand on it. Standing in the sand were a pair of ceremonial red candles and bunches of burning incense sticks. *Why do the candles have to be red?* On the card table were the dishes to be arranged in a precise pattern: five of everything—rice bowls, tea bowls (smaller and taller than the rice bowls), small and shallow wine bowls, chopsticks. *Why five and not four? Or six?*

I could hear sounds of the chopping cleaver on the thick cutting board as I walked in the door from school. The pungent smell of incense greeted me. I changed out of my uniform before reporting to the kitchen. With the afternoon sun and all the burners and oven on, the kitchen was sweltering. Mom had spent most of the day there preparing the required foods, and Marleen was already helping her. The chicken was cooked, chopped up and arranged in a bowl with its head and tail showing—evidence that a fresh, whole chicken had been cooked. Other traditional dishes included roast pork, a whole fish, tofu, shrimp, and vegetables like black mushrooms, ginkgo nuts, and bamboo shoots. *Why are there so many different dishes?*

Mom placed the heavy rice pot on the kitchen table. "Here, scoop the rice into the rice bowls, then set the table." I knew the rice had to be mounded neatly in a pleasing roundness. We didn't talk much as a general rule, but on feast days, we remained particularly focused to ensure the ceremonial details were correct and everything ready when Dad arrived home. I lined up the bowls in rows of five across the table near the incense box and placed the ivory chopsticks vertically in between the bowls. I did my best to remember where everything went, then poured tea into the tea bowls and gin into the wine bowls.

When Dad walked in the door, the table was ready. He spoke to Mom in Chinese and she responded. A yell of "Dad's home" brought everyone into the living room. A brother positioned floor pillows in front of the table. After setting aside his hat, jacket, and newspaper, Dad lit the candles, replaced the incense sticks with fresh ones. Next, he stood in front of the table, clasped his hands in front and bowed three times, knelt on the floor pillows and again bowed three times. Mom followed, then us, brothers first, according to age. We had been trained to show respect by being silent. It felt like playing follow-the-leader. No words of explanation or instruction, we simply mimicked the same movements. After we prayed, the incense continued burning while the ancestors ate. *How do they eat the food?* We waited, waving the flies away from the food until instructed to clear the table. The food was now blessed and ready for us to eat. *Are we eating their left-overs?* The food was cold from sitting so long. *Can we warm it up?*

So many questions. They were there, never to be spoken.

Chapter 4:
Seeing Red

Instructions for living a life: Pay attention.
Be astonished. Tell about it.
—Mary Oliver

Red refuses to be ignored. Its many permutations and shades capture my imagination. When signifying danger or caution or stop, it should be heeded. Red has shock value. It can dominate weaker colors. It exudes power and strength.

In Chinese culture, red represents good luck and happiness. Traditionally, brides wear red. Gifts of money are enclosed in red envelopes. Parties celebrating baby's one-month birthday require hard-boiled eggs dyed red.

In my childhood home in Honolulu, red punctuated our living spaces: a large cherry red upholstered chair and ottoman; a Naugahyde sofa, red like a Red Delicious apple, with component pieces that could be arranged together or apart; a chrome and Formica-topped kitchen table in a pattern of true red and brick red; kitchen floor tiles in a deep shade of maroon. The Chinese god of longevity, Shou Xing, stood against a vermillion background in a large embroidered picture on our living room wall.

Red is one of three primary colors. All other colors are created from red, yellow, and blue. Red appears at the top of the rainbow; it is the highest arc.

Red announces celebration and hope at holidays such as Christmas, Independence Day, Valentine's Day, Chinese New Year.

During my pre-school years, I could be happy with my coloring books all day long. One of my favorite crayons was magenta. Red danced a tango with blue and produced purple notes: Magenta was vibrant and sassy.

In stories, did red appear more frequently than any other color? It seemed so. Or maybe it just imprinted itself in my memory. Red Riding Hood, the

Little Red Hen, Alice's Red Queen, Rose Red, Dorothy's ruby slippers. As an older child, I would read *The Red Badge of Courage* and *The Scarlet Letter.*

Hawai'i's parades display such colorful pageantry. Each of the major islands is instantly recognizable with its designated color displayed on banner, horses, riders, and attendants walking alongside. Each island also has an official flower. Our newspapers and television stations covered the Aloha Week Parade every year. It was a major cultural event for local people that could last for hours. I was probably in my teens before joining a crowd along Kalākaua Avenue in Waikīkī to watch the parade, breathing in the air perfumed by real flowers decorating all the floats, clapping and cheering for each island unique in its own way.

Red would represent the Big Island of Hawai'i. A regal Hawaiian woman appeared on horseback in the parade. Riding sidesaddle, she wore the island's official color and flower: a red satin holokū with a long train flowing across the horse's flank and red lehua blossoms from the 'ōhi'a tree embellishing her black hair. Her lei and the horse's lei were also fashioned from lehua. This flower bursting with red rays appeared spiky, yet its petals were soft.

The color red also honors Pele, her fires of creation and destruction, her volcanoes, her power, her molten lava. Hawai'i, also known as the Big Island, is the youngest inhabited island, but the largest in land mass and still growing. Its active volcanoes, Kīlauea and Mauna Loa, continue to add acres of land. Seen from the air, the lava flows in fiery red rivers and streams against fields of older, hardened black lava. The fresh lava glows with heat and sends plumes of steam into the air when it meets any moisture, any water.

Red can mean life. It can mean death. It depends on whether blood is flowing within the body or pouring out of it.

~~~

I was nine years old. It was an ordinary warm and golden day, and I was outdoors on the swings with younger sister Joleen. Dad had driven off in his Buick sedan to work. The pavement near the house was wet from the early-morning watering he had given the flowering plants before leaving. The morning air carried a damp, earthy smell with hints of roses and pīkake (jasmine). I went into the house to the bathroom.

When I sat down on the toilet, I saw spots of blood on my panties. Where did this blood come from? What should I do? I couldn't think. I was numb with fear, but I decided to ignore it, hoping it was something random like a mosquito bite and would go away on its own. I changed my panties and went back outside to play. Later, when I again saw spots of blood, I could not contain my panic. I told Joleen, who of course knew less than I did and could say nothing helpful. I needed to tell somebody, to reassure myself this mysterious blood wasn't my imagination. I prayed the bleeding would stop. By afternoon, I examined my crotch to see if I had any cuts or injuries that might explain the bleeding. Bleeding was bad—I was old enough to know this—and it wasn't stopping.

The obvious struck me: I must be dying. A thrill raced through my body. Boy, everyone who's been mean to me will be so, so sorry! I started to make a mental list of those meanies... that's when fear reached out its sharp claws. I decided I had to cross the line and tell an adult. I needed to tell Mom.

I was nearly in tears, but her face revealed no emotion. "Come, let's go into the bathroom." She shut the door and locked it. She was very matter-of-fact, though not unkind.

"Take off your shorts and panties." She reached into a box on an upper shelf in the bathroom cabinet as I undressed. When she unwrapped the napkin, I saw a thick rectangular pad with two narrow ends that she attached to plastic clips on an elastic belt.

"Here's a sanitary belt and sanitary napkin." After her instructions, she delivered the unimaginable final words and informed me I would get a "period" every month. I would bleed *every* month for a few days. My brain froze and I cried inside: *No! This can't be! It doesn't make any sense. Why is my body doing this?* I wanted to scream, but said nothing. I simply listened and didn't question her.

It was clear that Mom was not surprised by the bleeding. Later, I recalled that during our annual physicals a few months ago, I saw her and the doctor talking quietly in the doctor's office after the exams—the measuring and weighing, the cold stethoscope on our backs, the immunizations. Then she joined us and we left. I guess he was advising her that my body was indicating signs of puberty.

This was my introduction to menstruation—such a life-changing moment in a girl's life. Little did I understand its significance at the time. Emotionally I was still a child as my body was becoming a woman's; I had no comprehension of this important transition. Mother-daughter discussions about this change and its implications did not exist in my family. A wall of silence so deep and so high, reinforced by untold generations, prevented us from talking about bodily functions and fluids. The following year when my mother became pregnant with my younger brother, I had no idea that menstruation was related to her condition. With little dialogue, explanation, or helpful advice from anyone, my body was expelling blood every month and, as far as I knew, for no good reason.

Innocently I thought my periods would continue to be the spotting of my first experience. When my pad revealed dark crimson on its pristine whiteness, I nearly fainted. Crimson became the color of humiliation. This body became alien. It was embarrassing. It was messy. Some days the blood flowed so heavily I felt it gushing from my body. I had bleed-throughs and found myself racing to the bathroom—how was I to know how often to change sanitary napkins?

Some months my body hurt with cramps that forced me to curl into a fetal position. Every month I learned what I could not control: physical discomfort, emotional turbulence, and practical inconvenience. I dreaded this unpredictable, unmentionable thing. The bulky pads and belt took up so much room in my small purse—what if they spilled out? Even worse, what if the bleeding showed on my outer clothes? Another dash to the girls' lavatory to wash out the stain. Or try to.

At home, I felt my face redden with impatience, disgust, and embarrassment as I saw the water in the sink turn reddish from my bloodied panties and sanitary belt. Red can mean anger: I felt like throwing them into the garbage; I wanted them and this bleeding to disappear from my life. Cleaning blood was difficult and hard work: even scrubbing and bleach did not eliminate all traces. Oh, it was stubborn! A brownish shadow remained to remind me of its power, of this new body I had not chosen or asked for. Even though I attended an all-girls school, I didn't know anyone else who was menstruating, not even sister Marleen, three years my senior.

Perhaps, being the first among the girls in my family to reach puberty broke some rules; older sister usually led the way—the first to go to school, to learn to hula, to get new clothes, which she would eventually pass down to me. My first bleeding was shocking. I was scared out of my mind, while Marleen felt upstaged when she found out. Clearly, this body had its own agenda, with no conscious intent on my part. I wish I could have felt some joy in being the first at something, even this. I didn't need to be treated like the women on the popular television show *Queen for a Day*, but I might have felt more positive if my naturally developing body hadn't been wrapped in secrecy. Menarche as a welcomed initiation into womanhood could have given me an entirely different sense of my body, my monthly bleeding, and becoming a woman.

~~~

Red is menses—from the Latin word mensis, meaning month. Exactly as my mother told me, the bleeding came every month. Unknown to me, my body could now create new life. No one seemed particularly alarmed. Red can mean life. It can mean death. It depends on whether blood is flowing within the body or pouring out of it.

At nine years old, my bleeding didn't kill me, but I did experience a death: My limited sense of my body died. I gained a new awareness, a new vigilance, and a reluctant respect for my physical self; it was not predictable as I once had thought. I had always taken it for granted unless I was sick. Now I became alert to what was happening within this skin at least once a month; at first I didn't know when the blood would flow or what new sensation I might experience. Instead of being familiar and comfortable, my body became mysterious and inscrutable.

I felt like a freak at times until my monthly rhythm eventually became more predictable. For a few years I lived with ignorance and confusion. In junior high a physical education teacher demystified how and why my body was doing this. I felt both relief and amazement. I learned a new vocabulary: ovaries, fallopian tubes, uterus, embryo. While I had the words, my understanding was still rudimentary. I learned that female bodies normally changed at age twelve or older, and not at nine. I was an early bloomer, ahead of the curve—lucky me! Still, I felt some comfort in knowing that having a period wasn't random or punitive. Instead, this was a natural course (not curse) in the physical development of girls. In fact, keeping a calendar of when I was bleeding every month revealed a pattern for when my period would start—what a revelation! I started feeling even less freakish when I realized that all girls on the planet went through this; every single one of us would experience a monthly bleeding. Some girls in my class had not started yet, but I knew what it was like. I was the experienced one.

However, this smugness, this confidence came later. Initially, my menstruating body set me apart from my peers and my sisters. I felt awkward and alone. Unfortunately, feeling different from others was nothing new to me. I sometimes wondered if I might be adopted. Dad's consistent favoritism toward his sons were like gut punches. They underscored being different, a layer of difference based on gender.

And now this: The biology of my body defined a new line. I crossed— actually, got pushed across—some kind of border into new unfamiliar territory. There was still so much I didn't know. Somehow I knew this: There was no going back.

Chapter 5:
1959

The farther backward you can look,
the farther forward you are likely to see.
— Winston S. Churchill

I t was an historic year. For some, a long-held dream became reality. Since 1893 Hawai'i has changed its political identity from kingdom to republic to a territory of the United States. Finally, in 1959, Congress voted to admit Hawai'i as the fiftieth state. The Senate approved the bill in March, followed by the House of Representatives. In August, President Dwight D. Eisenhower signed the Hawai'i Admission Act. After this, the festivities began.

And party we did. A Dixieland band marched in the streets of Waikīkī, shops closed their doors and declared a holiday, teenagers danced on the grounds of 'Iolani Palace, and free statehood celebrations featured local entertainers, Hawaiian music, and hula dancers. A festive cacophony filled the air: bells ringing from churches, whistles and foghorns blasting from ships and boats, horns honking from cars in traffic.

None of this, however, could compare with nature's show. One day in December, we woke up to the news that Kīlauea on the Big Island of Hawai'i had erupted in a magnificent show of lava fountains geysering up from Kīlauea Iki crater. This was living proof of the legendary Madame Pele, an introduction to her power.

Whether the dramatic eruptions revealed Pele's opinion about statehood was anyone's guess. Proponents might have said, "Sure, it's a sign of support. It's celebratory like fireworks." Chinese families like mine customarily burned firecrackers for good luck. The racket, sounding like machine guns, was supposed to chase away harmful spirits. However, opponents would have disagreed: "No, this is a sign of displeasure, this is Pele's fury."

The fiery lava fountains reaching record-breaking heights of 1,900 feet overwhelmingly surpassed even the most elaborate fireworks display. This new lava eventually added a layer of 390 feet to the old crater floor. Activity ended on December 21, but less than a month later, lava flows resumed. This time it destroyed the village of Kapoho, twenty-eight miles away, and flowed toward the ocean creating 500 acres of new land on the coastline. Nearly every year since 1959, red lava has flowed on the Big Island, reinforcing Pele's presence and power while garnering her new respect.

~~~

More significantly for my family, 1959 was a watershed year. Dad had a serious heart condition. In late 1958, he had to have surgery. We kids knew he was in the hospital, but couldn't visit him and were kept ignorant of the details. We instinctively knew Dad's health was precarious even though words like "death" and "dying" didn't occur to us; at least I wasn't aware of any serious concern among my siblings. Although we weren't noisy or rambunctious, we strove to be quieter and more thoughtful when Dad came home from the hospital.

Dad realized the urgency to change his lifestyle and reduce stress in his life, so he committed to drastically changing his diet to decrease saturated fats and manage his hypertension, taking vitamins along with his medications, and practicing t'ai chi each morning and evening. Over time, he lost weight, regained his health, and resumed his normal activities. When he returned to work, I vaguely remember he initially worked shorter hours. In the early months of 1959, Mom became pregnant, producing a new son in November. With this seventh child, Harry, we were as many as the seven inhabited islands of Hawai'i. From north to south, they are Ni'ihau, Kaua'i, O'ahu, Moloka'i, Lana'i, Maui, and Hawai'i. I turned 10 years old in 1959; the oldest sibling was 17 and the youngest, nine, excluding our new brother.

Life for me felt irrevocably different after Harry's birth. He was definitely a surprise. I wonder if Mom had had early signs of menopause, which caused her to believe her child-bearing days were over. Or did she mistakenly believe that after the age of 40, she automatically became barren? I liked reading Mom's magazines—*McCall's*, *Ladies Home Journal,* and *Redbook*—and cannot recall any articles about women's bodies and "the change of life." No one wrote to Dear Abby with such questions.

As an older child, I didn't completely understand that Harry's arrival could and would disrupt the family. Nor that my parents were highly distracted with the coming of this late-in-life child. Dad was nearly 60 years old; he was proud of his virility and took credit for producing not only another healthy child, but another son! Who could imagine such great fortune? It's as if Dad had given birth, not Mom. However, given his recent life-threatening heart attack, Dad bestowed special significance on Harry's birth. Dad felt renewed and revitalized, but what about Mom? What did she feel after the uncertainty of her husband's surgery and the possibility of being a widow with six children? And now here was an additional child and no guarantee about the future health of her husband. Nevertheless, she didn't display any worry and welcomed all the attention focused on this new son. Visitors came to see him and brought gifts. He was clearly the star while I and my siblings were pushed off-stage except when help was needed.

This usurper generated mixed feelings for me. I wanted to be helpful, but resentment kept rearing up. These changes did not come with instructions for dealing with the further diminishment of my life. My three older brothers were self-sufficient and didn't require any help from me, but Harry did, so I was expected to "serve" his needs, as if he were a little Buddha. His presence dominated the home: his crying, bottles and formula in the kitchen, piles of diapers and baby clothes to launder. Still, having a new baby in the house was beyond exciting, especially in that first year. He was adorable and wondrous—a great source of entertainment. For a while, all he did was lie in his crib, a warm bundle needing constant attention. His personality started emerging; he was happy and playful. He recognized me and probably thought my sole purpose was to entertain him. Suddenly he was standing up in his crib, next crawling on the floor. While fascinating, he was also exhausting. Mom shouldered the brunt of the work, but she expected her three daughters to be ever-ready to help; babies demanded a lot of work and time. We were in training for Future Moms of America.

~~~

On a typical weekend day, I would be sitting on my bed, leaning against the wall with a book in my lap. When my hand reached down, I felt the rows of soft tufts of fabric that ran horizontally across the faded blue chenille bedspread. The window to the right of me would be open to let the light morning breeze freshen the room. The sheer drapes billowed across my face. I pushed them away.

My solitude was broken when my mother called, "Come help me with the laundry." I lay down on my stomach engrossed in the story. She called again, a little louder, "Loreen, come hang up the laundry!" Continuing to read, I told myself, *I'll stop as soon as I finish this chapter.* Time passed as I traveled into the world on the pages. The room with its two twin beds, a high chest of drawers and closet, my family, the entire house and everything in it completely disappeared.

My mother came to the door of the bedroom. Since my back faced the door, I didn't see her. She walked over to the bed and grabbed the book out of my hands. I moved to take it back, but she was bigger even though I was tall for my age. "Now, go and hang the laundry!"

I had no choice and stomped out of the room, through the living room, and out the kitchen door. I slipped into my flip-flops and went down a few steps to the laundry room. I could feel my face getting flushed, but the sooner I completed this chore, the sooner I could get back to my book. I pulled the clothes out of the washing machine and into a round aluminum bucket, then carried it out to the clothesline.

I grabbed one towel and pinned the short end of one corner to the line, then took another towel and joined its corner to the one hanging there. I attached the two corners with one clothespin, one by one until all the towels were hanging—rectangle pastels—in the sunshine. Being outside among the clean laundry actually felt good. The fresh air. The warm sun. The smell of newly washed towels and clothing.

The washing machine was starting again. The sloshing of the clothes in the wash cycle probably included baby clothes and diapers. Washing baby clothes seemed endless. There was no escaping—more laundry would need hanging. I sighed, went to find my book, and sat on the steps to read, waiting for the next load.

~~~

Ready or not, 1959 ushered in a new beginning, a transition into unimaginable events for my island home. Statehood was only a prelude to the vast changes on the horizon. Being ten, I was grounded in the present without the capacity to contemplate the future. Altering the family status quo, the new baby was plenty to deal with. Our house only had three bedrooms, so it was tight quarters enough for eight people, much less nine. My existence revolved around home, school, studying, chores, helping with the baby. Outside this bubble, I had no hint how much all our lives would change.

Vineyard Street, the quiet little street where we lived, transformed when it became Vineyard Boulevard with four lanes of traffic. Our driveway had to be shortened, while our rental houses were moved closer together as our property shrank to accommodate the state's transportation demands. All along Vineyard, for many blocks, private property lines were redrawn.

We witnessed other changes that blew into the island. In 1957, millionaire-industrialist Henry J. Kaiser constructed the Hawaiian Village Hotel and built a geodesic dome of silvery aluminum, a landmark showroom we referred to as the Kaiser Dome. He later developed Hawai'i Kai, a huge residential and commercial development near Koko Head. Also, in 1957, a huge shopping mall broke ground across from Ala Moana Beach. The first phase of Ala Moana Shopping Center opened in 1959 anchored by Sears, Long's Drugs, and Foodland.

Before the new shiny shopping center opened with endless parking spaces, everyone went shopping downtown. Only a few blocks from the downtown core, Chinatown also prospered with steady customers. When retail customers began shopping more and more at the shopping center, downtown and Chinatown businesses suffered. Many were small businesses like Dad's store. Financial pressures on Dad must have been enormous during these years, thus providing the context for Dad's irritability and stress although we kids had no awareness of such troubles. Like everyone, we were excited about the new shopping center without understanding how our family's finances might be impacted. We'd gone to the grand opening, walking around and gawking at all the merchandise in the huge new Sears. Long's Drugs stores began popping up all over the island. We took our film for development and got our medicines there. When Long's started selling many Asian foods and items, people shopped there and less frequently in Chinatown.

The second phase of Ala Moana was completed in 1966 when I was in high school. Downtown was more convenient for the sparse amount of shopping I had to do, but I felt lucky to get summer retail jobs at the new shopping center, which became a major attraction for tourists.

The island's physical landscape continued to transform post-statehood. Even though these changes were obvious, I remained oblivious to its economic shifts. In 1959, the economy still depended on sugar and pineapple. When jet planes were introduced, the airlines began offering affordable fares, which dramatically increased tourism to the islands. Major airlines vied for routes to Honolulu after statehood. Within a few years, tourism became the major industry supporting the state's economy. Investors built more hotels to accommodate tourists coming from all over the world. Large and small businesses catering to these visitors thrived. Real estate development boomed and local millionaires were born. Since islands have limited land, developers began building skyward to offer more condos, apartments, offices. High-rise towers became ubiquitous as panoramic scenic views dwindled. Inevitably, property values increased everywhere, leaving locals to wonder if they could ever afford to purchase their own homes or even remain in the islands. Many moved away.

It was a cascading effect. More tourists created more businesses that created more jobs that attracted new residents, increasing the population and demand for more housing. Real estate development, both residential and commercial, continued to boom. For years, the entire city seemed to be under construction with new hotels, highways, and a bigger airport to accommodate both international and domestic travelers.

None of this was evident in 1959 when we were still a small, intimate island community. None of this would have concerned a ten-year-old immersed in her books, family dramas, the mysteries of her body, and the quiet turmoil of adjusting to a newborn in the home.

Chapter 6:
No Words

One does not become enlightened by imagining figures of light,
but by making the darkness conscious.

—Carl Jung

nother component to Daddy's new health regimen is weekly massages at home. Sometimes Mrs. Nojima provides the massages and other times it's Mr. Kishi. They go into the courtyard and shut the doors. I am curious: *What are they doing? What is a massage?*

One day, when Daddy is leaving the room after his massage, he sees me hovering near the door. "Come and see what it's like. Mr. Kishi can give you a sample." Daddy is smiling and I'm not sure if he's serious, but I'm always ready to please Daddy, happy for his attention. I enter the courtyard. The sharp, clean smell of liniment permeates the room. While Daddy is in his bedroom, I'm alone in the courtyard with Mr. Kishi. He invites me to lie down on the mattress, kneels down next to me, says softly, "OK, relax...you going feel sleepy. Listen to my voice. Your eyes feel heavy. I going count to ten and you sleep when I reach ten. One...two...three...." As he counts, I yawn and close my eyes. I can still hear his voice when he reaches ten. I'm not really asleep, but I play along thinking this is a game. He mutters something in Japanese. He unbuttons my blouse and puts his mouth on my just-budding breasts. I keep my eyes closed as I've been instructed.

He gets up and moves to my feet. His hands are unzipping my shorts, then pulling down my shorts and panties. I feel his hand between my legs. Suddenly I feel his finger inside my body. *Am I imagining this?* I'm not familiar with this part of my body. I know I'm not imagining this. This is real: He put his finger inside me. My mind is racing. *It doesn't hurt, but what is he doing?* I feel an unaccustomed pressure there. I don't know what to do. If I should do something. If this is something bad. I can't figure this out. It doesn't make sense. I can't make any sense of it.

I don't remember if he says anything. I don't think so. My own thoughts are so loud inside my head, so frantic that I'm aware of little else.

I am in my home. My parents are in the house. They invited this man here. He is helping Daddy. Thoughts like these ping-pong around in my head. We all want Daddy to get better. Although we have no details—his condition is not discussed—we know it's serious. Some minutes later, I hear Mr. Kishi talking again, telling me to wake up.

My thoughts flee. I open my eyes and get up in a cloud of uncertainty. My clothes are back the way they should be. I am not physically hurt. I have no physical evidence of harm—no bruises, no bleeding, nothing broken. So, what is this feeling that something is wrong?

He's calm as if nothing has happened, as if he did nothing wrong. That's how I know he really believes he hypnotized me with his mumbo-jumbo and that I don't know what he did. He's right. I'm not sure what happened. At any rate, he doesn't have to warn me not to tell anyone.

And I don't. I don't have the words to describe what happened. I had so little knowledge about my body. I barely touched my own body and had no awareness of its secrets. Back then, we trusted everyone who came into our home, and if my father suggested we do something, we felt confident in doing so. I had no reason to distrust adults, to be wary of them inflicting harm.

However, my discomfort persists, nags at me like an annoying hangnail. Or like someone insisting the sky is yellow when I can see for myself it's blue. As in the past, like when I danced in kindergarten, I know I have to figure this out on my own. *Must not bother the adults. It's probably nothing anyway.* I try to reassure myself. Still, I cannot ignore the soft clanging of an internal alarm.

On return visits to the house, Mr. Kishi calls me over and I can't say no. He is an adult and we do not disobey adults. And I am a good girl. If I am menstruating, he puts my clothes back on when he sees my sanitary napkin and leaves me alone down there.

Before long, I somehow acquire some gumption, some courage. The next time he calls to me, I let my body speak: I shake my head no, turn my back and walk away in the opposite direction.

Amazingly, I defy an adult and the world does not fall off its axis.

This is how it ends. Or so I think.

Part 2: Wahine
(Woman)

Chapter 7:
Forgetting and Loss

The real difficulty is to overcome how you
think about yourself.
—Maya Angelou

In Hawai'i, the land is alive. Volcanoes manifest vitality by spilling glowing red lava down the mountains. Or exploding fountains of lava toward the sky. Mana is another manifestation of the land's life energy. If one is tuned in to the land, one can feel it pulsating like a heartbeat or an electric current. It's a life force that resonates in one's bones. Whether walking or sitting quietly, one will notice that some locations emit stronger vibrations than others.

Aloha 'āina means love for the land. The land is sentient. Sacred. The powerful goddess of fire and Hawaiian volcanoes, Madame Pele, is creator. The Hawaiians love their islands, respect all living things. Even rocks, or pōhaku, have life or mana. All are progeny of Pele.

Visitors to the Big Island of Hawai'i see fields of black and gray lava rock, visit inactive volcanoes like Mauna Kea, look into the caldera of Mauna Loa, even see lava flowing into the ocean on the southeastern coast of the island. The transformative power of Pele is evident everywhere.

And yet, many visitors and non-Hawaiians don't believe. They don't believe the warnings posted everywhere in Hawai'i Volcanoes National Park: DO NOT TAKE LAVA ROCKS OR REMOVE ANYTHING FROM THE PARK. You will be breaking the law if you do so. However, the Federal Government is not the only entity to fear. Believe me, you don't want to mess with Pele. Taking a piece of lava for a souvenir is an act of disrespect to her. It is stealing from this goddess who created these islands, these mountains, land, beaches.

Volcanoes are Pele's special domain, and all the many forms of lava

55

belong to her: black sand, bits of Pele's tears or hair—lava that the wind has caught and shaped into small shiny pieces or spun into fine strands—and olivine, a common mineral in Hawaiian lava that forms olive-green crystals when lava cools; all belong to Pele. It's not about property ownership. These are intrinsic parts of her. Taking one rock is taking a piece of Pele. It is dismembering her body.

The park has many prominent exhibits at the visitor center. One is a display of items taken in the past with authentic letters written by remorseful visitors who chronicle their stories of bad luck and even tragedy since returning home: death, divorce, accidents, illness, losses of every kind. They enclose the items taken with apologies to Pele and hope that restoring these items to the park will end their misery.

Many label these events as Pele's Curse. Consider this: How would *you* like to have a part of *your* body, *your* being removed without consent, simply taken? How would *you* like it if someone violated *your* body?

~~~

Nothing seemed amiss. My girlhood continued and I officially became a teenager at thirteen. I liked rock 'n roll music, but Elvis held no charm for me. Other teenagers and women swooned when he sang and swiveled his hips. Not me. My heart fluttered for Ricky Nelson and Bobby Rydell. Joining a record club gave me options to indulge in Sinatra and Broadway musical soundtrack albums. I loved the old movie musicals shown on television with all that dancing and singing featuring Judy Garland, Gene Kelly, Eleanor Powell, Ginger Rodgers, and Fred Astaire. I adored the newer ones, too: *The Sound of Music, My Fair Lady,* and *West Side Story*—such romance, such music!

What I heard at home also influenced my taste in music. My father was a fan of Bing Crosby and Nat King Cole. Brother Clyde listened to classical music and Tom became a huge fan of bossa nova: the Brazilian songs of Antonio Carlos Jobim, jazz renditions by Stan Getz, and the breathy voice of Astrid Gilberto singing "The Girl from Ipanema." When the Beatles hit the scene, all other music took a backseat. My classmates and I got swept up by these Brits, with their upbeat music, lyrics I could actually hear and understand, and long hair. The Fab Four changed pop music during my teen years and reinforced my romantic inclinations with their many love songs.

I dated when I was sixteen and had fun, but romance never came calling, much less announced itself with orchestral music.

Older girls from my school left the islands for mainland colleges. I listened rapturously to their stories when they visited, almost turned green when I heard about their new lives. I dreamed of following their lead and looked into the future at my sparkling new life. I needed a glimpse of myself as my own person. Going away to college appealed to the adventurous, individualistic spirit in me, so I invested my whole self into making it happen. Academics was the easy part. Broadening my scope in extracurricular activities and demonstrating leadership qualities, I held this dream close and fast from age sixteen. However, I did not fully comprehend my father's gender bias nor his financial constraints.

The financial realities of such an education were enormous: tuition, books, school fees, living expenses, airfare during holidays and in the summer. Plus, there were six of us siblings just a year or two apart and all being groomed for college. These details escaped me as I watched Ben and Tom go off to St. Mary's College in California and naïvely thought, *If they can do it, so can I.* Disappointment did not appear as a possibility on my horizon.

Looking forward to graduation in 1967, I set my sights high; Mills College and Claremont College, both respected private schools in California, accepted me. I was elated with this enormous validation. Overflowing with confidence and grand optimism, I felt my reward within reach. My biggest challenge seemed deciding which school to accept.

With the deadline approaching for responding to the schools, Dad calmly wrecked my life by telling me: I had to decline both colleges and attend the University of Hawai'i. I was stunned and devastated—this should have been my ticket for leaving home, for changing my life. I longed for something different. Without fully recognizing the source of this yearning, I knew I had to get away. I simply *had to.*

Dad's words were final. He didn't explain why. He didn't have to. Clearly, I wasn't good enough. Bitter, hot tears flowed and could not be contained. As if I had been struck, I cried like a toddler: wailing and sobbing—my body racked with a pain so deep, so bitter, and seemingly endless. I crashed on my bed. *Why had he let me apply to these schools?* It seemed utterly cruel and unforgivable. I became pure emotion, an open wound. With eyes puffy and red, I lost the ability to speak, my sobs washing over any words and rendering them incoherent. I felt darkness. I grieved the loss of my dream, of the imagined future I never doubted, that seemed more real than I even suspected. A sorrow without any bottom. Was it day or night? How long had

I been crying? One day or two? Nothing mattered.

Most of all, it was so unfair. So UNFAIR! More tears. Would I ever recover? Why should I? I had no future. What kind of life would that be? With a dark void staring at me, I could find little reason to live. Maybe I could just sink into that darkness and disappear.

Of course, here too I was thwarted: I did not die. Instead, I grudgingly enrolled at the University of Hawai'i and continued living at home. By the time college started months later, reason had somewhat returned and I tried making the best of things.

No, it wasn't over. Feelings about my parents bubbled to the surface—I let myself feel anger for the first time. I was supposed to be an obedient daughter, not an angry one. Even though I did not display this anger, I felt it in my body. Blood simmering, constantly on the verge of boiling over. Throat aching with suppressed screams. Head throbbing with words I couldn't say. This anger could not be ignored and was directed at Dad. He had not prepared me for this possibility as I blithely completed the applications and he carefully filled out the financial aid forms. He provided no reality check to my dreams, no helpful commentary or guidance on possible outcomes. I felt betrayed; I had done my part by working hard, really hard by earning outstanding grades, being involved in a variety of extra-curricular activities, taking leadership roles, and getting impeccable reference letters from teachers. Maybe I should have been smart enough to figure out the family's financial situation for myself, but I wasn't. Dad kept all family financial matters to himself. Even though there had been no explicit bargain, no agreement except in my mind, this feeling of betrayal persisted.

My eyes opened wide to the reality that I would never be as good as my brothers. Dad had condemned me to this reality. My eyes also narrowed in rage. Being a good girl and an obedient daughter meant nothing. Being on the honor roll meant nothing. Being a boy was *everything*. They did not have to earn their rewards. Their world was unlimited; my father's support for their needs was assumed, never in question—all because they were male.

Years later, Mom told me that Dad couldn't send me away to school because Marleen had gone to the University of Hawai'i, and I couldn't have something that wasn't given to her. I was dumbfounded. Instead of mollifying me, this information further incensed me. Such rationale was completely bogus because Clyde had also attended the local university, yet his younger brothers went off to school in California. Inside, I was stomping around and screaming, throwing the tantrums that were not permitted. This anger mostly simmered for a long, long time—burning below the surface. My trust and respect for my father plummeted. Meanwhile, life continued onward and my life appeared normal—teenage angst and all.

Except life really wasn't. I had lost a piece of myself when I was ten. No, I hadn't it lost: It had been taken, stolen, killed. During these years I didn't have conscious memory of what happened in our home's courtyard. It was as if a giant hand had wiped away this memory. At ten, I was too young to understand the magnitude of this man's actions, too young to process the violation and violence against me. Yet, some inner wisdom—perhaps a guardian angel or protective ancestor—stepped in to lift this away or somehow make it invisible to my young self, to my conscious mind.

This loss of memory, while a saving grace, created a hole in my personhood—a lost self, a lost innocence, a loss of wholeness so deep that even now I cannot begin to fathom its depth, so dark that I fear being plunged into eternal night.

Maybe my young girl-self exhibited some clues. I don't remember. Perhaps my smile became more tentative. Or I carried myself differently. Or my personality shifted ever so slightly, becoming quieter or more vocal. If so, no one said a thing.

No wonder. Being a girl was of little consequence.

Still, my body had recorded what happened and stored these memories.

One day in fifth grade, I couldn't see what was on the blackboard in the classroom. I moved closer to the front of the room. After my teacher informed my parents, I received my first pair of glasses to correct the myopia.

At the time I thought it was cool to wear glasses; all my older siblings wore glasses and I felt like one of them. But no, there was no entry into their world. In retrospect, I wonder if my body was trying to send me a message. Was it hinting that something evil had happened—something I wasn't ready to see? That it was okay to hide behind these unflattering lenses, to be unattractive? Did my body provide other clues about my terrible secret?

No one knew or suspected that something was horribly, horribly wrong. Not even me.

Chapter 8:
Love and Other Misunderstandings

We love because it is the only true adventure.
—Nikki Giovanni

In 1967 I was eighteen, perched on the cusp of adulthood and anxious to test my wings. I had recently graduated from St. Andrew's Priory, a small all-girls school I'd attended since fourth grade.

The University of Hawai'i signified a totally different galaxy: a huge campus of 320 acres and co-ed classes, some of them in lecture halls as large as auditoriums. I encountered young men from different races and backgrounds. However, romance remained elusive. This wasn't my sole reason for going to college of course. I was so impatient for a different life after many years of being cloistered and repressed by parents, nuns, teachers.

I sensed a low-grade, barely discernible sense of urgency in the air, like a constant static. The conflict in Vietnam was dividing the country. It divided families. The futures of young men hung in the balance as the draft determined who to send into war. Men burned their draft cards. Anti-war demonstrations erupted across the country, while student activists spoke out passionately on college campuses, including the University of Hawai'i. The 1967 Summer of Love could not halt the war machine.

In Honolulu, there was a noticeable increase in military personnel on the streets. Even out of uniform, their closely-cropped heads identified them as soldiers. Our university campus and city streets were less volatile than other places in the news. We were insulated by our location, with thousands of miles of ocean between us and the nearest continent, and yet as the closest American soil to Asia, we became enmeshed in the war machinery. I focused on being the good student my parents expected since I was not equipped to handle, much less understand, the nightly news that brought the war into our living rooms, scenes filled with ground and air combat, bombs and napalm, body bags, and news reporters dressed in camouflage. Why were we over there? Why were we sacrificing American lives? I was young and too self-absorbed to make a concerted effort to comprehend the gravity of the war, the politics, and Hawai'i's role in Pacific wars.

Instead, here's what caught my attention: A notice in the local newspaper about the upcoming Marine Corps 192nd Birthday Ball stated MARINES WANT DATES; PLEASE CALL THIS NUMBER. That sounded fun! And I'd be doing a public service. After I called and left my number, my heart hammered in my chest as if I'd been running. I longed for some excitement in my predictable and dull life.

A week or two went by. Nothing. No one was going to call. I returned my attention to school and studying and had almost forgotten about it when I received a phone call from a Marine.

I arrived early at the Armed Forces YMCA in downtown for our meeting. I looked around. Little activity and few people. I was the only local young woman so he could not possibly miss me. On the phone he told me he was stationed at Camp H.M. Smith located in Hālawa Heights between downtown Honolulu and Pearl Harbor. As I waited in the quiet lobby, I wondered if this meeting was a mistake. I could leave and no one would ever know. I looked up and saw a tall young man dressed neatly in slacks and an orange short-sleeved plaid shirt striding toward me. He had a boyish, clean-shaven face and broad shoulders.

Rick was so far removed from my background with his blond and blue-eyed Scandinavian looks that I liked him immediately. I was tanned to a shade resembling almond butter and had straight, long black hair, very Asian eyes, high cheekbones, and an insignificant nose. After the initial hellos, we walked to a cafe.

At first, we were both shy and a bit wary, like animals of different species might be. I broke the ice. "My family's Chinese. You're Scandinavian, right?"

"Yeah, we're Danes. My hometown is full of Danes and Germans. Do you know Lake Erie? The town's near the lake."

"No Asian people?"

"That's right."

I wasn't really surprised, but couldn't help thinking he was really from white-bread America. Curiosity definitely factored into our attraction to each other.

I jumped to another question. "Do you like being in the Marines?"

"It's okay. I'm seeing places I might never get a chance to see. First California and now here."

"And Honolulu—do you like it here?"

"It's a little overwhelming for me. I grew up in a small town and this is a big city compared to where I'm from. And it's tropical...I thought San Diego was tropical, but.... I'm still really exploring the island. And just got a car. Maybe you can show me around?"

I smiled, unsure of what to say.

He filled in the silence. "The beaches and ocean are great! It's the first time... I'm used to swimming in pools and lakes, but ocean-swimming is really great. Very different. I couldn't believe how warm the water is. I wrote my parents and told them all about it."

I glanced away. He obviously liked swimming. "I should tell you something. I don't go to the beach very often. And...," I cleared my throat and looked down. "And I never learned to swim."

"I don't believe you. Really?" I felt his eyes on me.

"Really. I know. It's kinda embarrassing, but it's true."

"Wow." He paused. "Not a problem. I assumed everyone here went swimming. Could swim automatically. All this beautiful water—how could you not?"

I shrugged. "My parents didn't send us to swimming classes. It's not required in the schools, and besides my school didn't even have a pool." I told him how my parents emphasized education and good grades. They encouraged us to develop our minds. Not so much sports or athletics, although my brothers casually pursued sports like tennis and softball.

We both relaxed and talked for more than an hour. I learned that, with an older brother and younger sister, Rick was a middle child like me. Along with most people in town, his dad worked for the tire factory. His mom was a housewife. He liked rock and roll, especially the Righteous Brothers. For him, the best thing about high school was competing on the swim team. That explained his broad shoulders.

Then reality reared up: *Uh-oh, I have to tell my parents. I have to tell them I've met a Marine and agreed to go to the Marine Corps Ball.*

They. Were. Not. Happy. I could see it in their faces, which paled as their mouths turned down, unable to remain neutral. In shock, they averted their eyes. Mom glanced quickly at Dad to gauge his reaction.

Not much for words, my father finally asked, "You just met him? He's haole? And he's a *Marine*?"

I responded affirmatively. Unspoken, these words hung in the air: How could you do this? He's a stranger, someone whose background and family are unknown and cannot be verified. Stupid girl!

My four older siblings were dating appropriate Chinese boys and girls, all raised in the islands and on the college track. While I knew my parents preferred we date Chinese, I did not know how strongly they felt about us dating non-Chinese. Or I didn't want to know.

I knew the Vietnam conflict was controversial and escalating. Still, I didn't comprehend the bigger picture. In Vietnam, young white men like Rick were killing Asian people, who looked like me and my family. Also, Camp Smith, where Rick was stationed, was headquarters for the Commander In Chief, Pacific Command. The highest-ranking, top military brass overseeing all armed forces operating in the Pacific Rim frequented Camp Smith to strategize war operations.

Dad insisted on meeting Rick. Not an unreasonable request, although he had never screened my dates before. The meeting occurred a few days before the ball. I was nervous. Even though Rick had survived boot camp, meeting my Dad could make any Marine doubt his own toughness.

The day of their meeting, Rick was a young foreigner with a questionable passport to our Hawaiian-Chinese lifestyle. Clearly visible were several porcelain vases and bowls, some painted with scenes and people from ancient times, scrolls and other Chinese decorations marked with calligraphy, and a wool carpet with an Oriental design. The only item in the living room that was typically American was the television.

My siblings made themselves scarce. Across the room from where Dad and Rick sat, Gung Gung Lee and Po Po Lee, unsmiling in big-as-life photographic portraits, witnessed the proceedings. These portraits of my grandparents remained in the same place on the same wall throughout my life and acquired corporeal significance. They watched over the family, especially us children—on the right, Po Po in a Chinese traditional dress with hair smoothed back into a bun and on the left, Gung Gung in a three-piece Western suit. Their eyes looked stern and admonishing, their gazes penetrating and inescapable.

I sat with my back to them, thankfully avoiding their eyes.

A large picture of the Chinese god of longevity, Shou Xing, hung on the wall facing the front door. Wearing traditional robes, this god dominated a vermillion background. His presence was impossible to miss.

Rick was up against more than my parents. He was surrounded by an entire community, guardians of the culture in the flesh and in spirit.

My father's conduct was formal, his voice more gruff than necessary. They shook hands, and Dad invited Rick to sit. My 60-ish, serious father and a blond, buff young man sat on the hard koa-wood chairs near the screened windows in the living room. With furrowed forehead, Dad leaned back and narrowed his eyes to scrutinize Rick as he spoke. We served tea, but it did not bring warmth into the meeting. Mom and I sat quietly on the sidelines as the interrogation commenced. Dad hoped to uncover something objectionable. Rick responded politely, directly, truthfully.

"No, sir, I did not consider going to college."

"Yes, sir, I enlisted."

"Sir, my rank is lance corporal."

Of course, I had only recently met Rick myself and didn't really know if there was anything in his background that might be less than honorable. He struck me as a clean-cut, all-American guy with little or no pretensions.

After the meeting once Rick had left, my father was still reluctant. He asserted his authority, "You can go to the ball, but that's it. You will not see him again."

I breathed out in relief, not listening to the finality of his words. I felt like Cinderella and wanted to shout, I'm going to the ball! I'm going to the ball!

~~~

Honestly, that's all I expected at the time. Rick picked me up on the evening of the ball. Stunningly handsome in his dress blues, he made quite an impression. I wore a cocktail-length, pale pink brocade dress. When we arrived at the Hickam NCO Club at Hickam Air Force Base, the room was full of young men all in their dark blue jackets with shiny brass buttons embossed with the U.S. Marine Corps insignia, white caps and white gloves—all spit and polish, gleaming and well-groomed. The military was an unfamiliar universe, but I had attended a number of formal and semi-formal events in high-school. We had cocktails and dinner, then danced all night. I don't remember what we ate or the evening's program or what we talked about. When we danced, he held me in his arms and I leaned into his broad shoulders. They felt protective and strong. I wanted that protection. I wanted his strength. Simple as that, I fell in love.

My father had set a curfew, which we honored. Although the event included a buffet breakfast at 2 a.m., I was safely home by midnight, like Cinderella. It was a lovely evening and I never doubted I would see Rick again. It would not be easy, but I was determined. I was in college after all; I was nearly an adult and could handle myself and make my own decisions. I had to start thinking for myself sometime, didn't I?

I defied my father's injunction—behavior that was previously unthinkable. Being in love made me feel I could do anything. Our meetings were clandestine, like Tony and Maria in *West Side Story*. Rick met me after my classes were over for the day. I didn't drive, so Rick picked me up in his older model Corvair, sporty with bucket seats and trim style—a fine car for getting around.

We went to the beach or drove away from the city. Holding hands and kissing escalated to embracing each other closely, tightly. Our passion evolved over time into finding a place to park at night. In Honolulu, one popular place was Magic Island, property created by landfill for the expansion of Ala Moana Beach Park. Magic Island, with the dark, star-filled sky above and the ocean beyond and the wind whispering in the palm trees—most nights here were full of parked cars with teenagers eager for love and exploring each other's bodies.

I traveled with Rick into these uncharted waters and blew open my then-limited world. Actually, we both fumbled around at first and willingly taught each other. Only a year older, he was a "near-virgin": He'd had only one girlfriend in high school; he told me they'd had sex once. Kissing became passionate kissing, French kissing. Embraces became caresses, our fingers seeking discovery of sensitive points on the body. Sighing became ragged breathing. Our clothes remained intact at first, but being in love, we let our hands explore below the layers into more intimate zones. Even with a stick shift separating the two bucket seats, our young bodies, flexible and eager and fueled by desire and surging hormones, met the challenge of touching and tasting. The mouth as a conduit for erotic pleasure—who knew? I was like a child learning to walk, stepping into a different way of understanding my body and myself.

I did not want to consummate our love in a car. I could not relax completely or be comfortable in this setting. Everyone knew this was a huge make-out scene, with police cars cruising the area frequently. No, this would not be the setting for losing my virginity. I required privacy and comfort. Also, without any recreational drugs, I felt already "stoned": I was grooving on the way my body tingled and the natural high of deep physical pleasure; I wasn't sure how much more I could handle. Female orgasm and knowledge of the G-spot had yet to enter my consciousness. Rick was a true prince. Even when his pleasure became painful, desperate for release, he did not become a bully or a brute.

Devoted to each other, we were certain we had found true love. Not that either of us had enough experience to know the difference between infatuation and love, between sexual attraction and love, between physical pleasure and love, and frankly, between lust and love. Now I understood the love scenes in movies: the heat of passion, the lingering looks, the heart flutters and day-dreaming about one's beloved, the tortured hours of not being together, the secret knowledge of carnal desire, the recollection of sensory memories—his touch, his smell, his taste, his voice—any or all of these together made me feverish, constantly distracting me when we were apart.

~~~

Military life was distinctly different from my own—this was not news to me. Officers based in Hawai'i preferred their children attend private schools, and my school had its share of military brats, which is what they called themselves. Near downtown, St. Andrew's Priory was a religious school run by Episcopalian nuns, who lived in a simple building next to the school. Each morning we filed into St. Andrew's Cathedral for chapel, including lay teachers and girls from elementary through high school. In the center of the courtyard, a coral cross about fifteen feet tall greeted everyone. The Priory was a well-respected school, established in 1867.

Every morning special buses made the rounds, picking up students living on military bases and dropping them off at Priory and other private schools. From Navy, Army, Marine, and Air Force families, these girls were different from us locals. They were sassy, outspoken, disrespectful to authority, "fast"—seeming to live life far more accelerated than we did or could even imagine. Most of these girls were extroverts and white—easy to identify and easy to befriend. They were accustomed to moving from place to place and wasted no time in fitting into new environments and making new friends. They traveled the world to places I had only seen on maps as their fathers moved up the ranks.

They all dated early (as young as fifth and sixth grade) and had or wanted boyfriends. They were artful and sophisticated with makeup and hair and had well-developed busts (cleavage!) that even our shapeless middy blouses could not conceal. They took more risks and challenged the rules—hiking up their skirts higher than we dared and smoking on campus. And not only cigarettes. When I was a junior, some seniors were suspended for smoking pot. They were scandalous, while I remained safe and chaste in all things, observing their antics with a touch of envy. Such boldness! They opened a window into a much different lifestyle than my own.

I felt they must have a secret knowledge about life. I wanted this knowledge that imbued them with supreme self-confidence. Whether these girls were still virgins was not as important as their understanding of the power of their sexuality. They flirted easily and acted overly familiar with our male teachers, some of whom did not discourage such attentions and maybe even provoked them. Nothing overt or sordid happened, as far as I know, but I detected a charge in the air, a silent crackling, during their conversations in class. I wonder now: Was there a connection between this precocious behavior among girls from military families and military life, rife with its masculine toughness and phallic iconography?

In high school, my sexual feelings and awareness of my body had remained under wraps—no light shawl, but a heavy woolen overcoat covering me from neck to below the knees like camouflage. Sure, I dated some and had girlish crushes, but I did not understand my body, certainly not as a conduit for sexual pleasure.

High school biology and physical education taught the basic mechanics of sexual intercourse in the context of the human reproductive system. Or how the human species reproduces. We learned clinical names for male organs and female organs, how millions of sperm enter a woman's body to fertilize the egg that becomes the fetus. Clinical, dry, not the least bit interesting. I wondered why sex was such a big deal. In retrospect, what I learned is that talking about sex makes most adults uncomfortable, which can justify dishonesty, or not telling the whole truth. There was absolutely no discussion about sensuality or emotions, about passion or desire in the body, and what happens in the body when such feelings arise. Nor how such powerful urges can override intelligence, reason, and good judgment. Apparently, we teens could not be entrusted with such secret, important information. Promiscuity and teen pregnancies might result. It was like being given a car without instructions on how to drive, the rules of the road, and being a responsible driver.

Teenagers and burgeoning sexuality are as inseparable as toast and butter. At eighteen, I felt I was missing something unknown, something vital for me to be complete and whole and fully alive—something I imagined most other young people had already experienced, that turned their lives into Technicolor while mine remained black-and-white. My virginity, while a burden I was willing to relinquish, was only a part of it. I further sensed that the body I lived in day in and day out still held wondrous mysteries and precious knowledge. It functioned well, but seemed apart from me.

As a child I had plenty of curiosity, but none about my body. Without knowledge about my anatomy, I felt even more removed when I started to menstruate. As a young woman in love, I had not suspected that I could feel so alive, so passionate; I had no idea how accurate the phrase "being turned on" was. With Rick, I experienced myself as an electric grid with a switch that sent currents of electricity into every cell. Surely I glowed when turned on. My own physiological responses were nothing short of amazing: Kisses on my face and neck registered in my groin. I discovered I occupied a different body entirely—a real woman's body, a woman awakened to her sexuality. Even though we had not yet slept together, Rick was my lover and liberator.

And so, when this golden Marine came into my life and made my body sing, turned me on to life, to a world unimagined inside me—I could not, would not let him go.

~~~

While war continued to escalate in Vietnam, personal battles at home commanded my attention. Feeling Dad was being completely unreasonable, I turned to Mom. I wanted to make her my ally, hoped she could influence Dad. I was clearly delusional to think this given the existing power dynamics, but I felt compelled to communicate with one of them. As another woman, she would surely understand.

I began writing down my feelings and leaving her letters. A few times, we actually sat together at the dining room table and talked—at least, I talked. She listened, which raised my hopes that she would intercede later with Dad on my behalf. We were all intimidated by him, but it didn't occur to me at the time that Mom might be too. She also had the wisdom to recognize I was rebelling for good reason. Although she could not intervene, she witnessed how controlling my father was and how he favored his sons.

I suspect Mom was a romantic. She loved movies and novels, especially those with Asian characters: *Love Is a Many-Splendored Thing, The World of Suzie Wong, Flower Drum Song, The Good Earth.* Unfortunately, so many Asian female characters came to tragic ends. Perhaps she hoped that the lack of romance in her life would *not* be replicated in mine. At the very least, she wanted more options for her daughters than she'd had.

I wonder if she'd read *From Here to Eternity,* the bestseller by James Jones. Assuming Jones wrote an accurate portrayal of the times, it's no wonder my parents were horrified with the idea of their daughter dating a serviceman. Set in pre-World War II Honolulu, the novel describes Army life at Schofield Barracks, the racist climate within the military that fed tensions between local islanders and the military; the dissolute behavior of off-duty servicemen, including shacking up with local women resulting in illegitimate children— all abandoned when the men shipped out; and forbidden love between an enlisted man and an officer's wife.

I was an emotional young woman, with so much pent up inside. My hormones raged against the family code of silence. I was hungry for life, anxious to break away from familial restraints, but I also felt guilty for such thoughts. Something unknown, still hidden inside me was ready to—what? I didn't know, but *something* lay coiled in there, waiting. Talk was difficult, but somehow the words left my mouth, sprang forth from me across the dining room table.

"I know you and Dad don't approve, but I hope *you* understand. I only want to date this boy. It's not like I'm going to marry him."

I don't remember if she said anything. I wasn't sure what she thought. Perhaps: *Where did this daughter get such boldness? I would never discuss such things with my mother. Didn't have anyone to open my heart to.* However, unlike me, she never deviated from what was expected of her, as far as I know.

Mom tried to support me in her own way. She connected my disappointment in not going away to college with my infatuation with Rick. I didn't know I was confused with all these new feelings about men and desire, that I wanted to be in love, but didn't understand what love was. I never witnessed any discussion about my relationship with Rick between my parents. They would have spoken in Cantonese as they often did when talking about issues related to us children, so I wouldn't have understood their words. She would not have disagreed directly with my father. Yet I can imagine her telling Dad something like, "You see. You should have let her go to college in California."

As usual, Dad and I never talked about the situation. He knew I continued to see Rick. He didn't like it, but he never said a word to me; clearly I had made up my mind and would not back down. I suppose he could have kicked me out of the house. Doing so might have proven to be more disastrous, might have thrown me irrevocably into Rick's arms. (Years later, I found out that strong-willed women run in the Lee family. Two of my aunts had defied my strict grandfather and dated men he disapproved of—men whom my aunts married.) Dad hoped and I'm sure prayed our relationship would run its course. Rick would eventually get his orders to ship out and that would end it.

In fact, Rick was stationed in Honolulu longer than we dared to dream. We dated for almost two years. While neither of us had much money, being in love in Honolulu came with perks that didn't require money, like walks along Waikīkī Beach at sunset. Spectacular colorations of purple, orange, gold, pink and red filled the clear tropical skies, then darkness romantically lit by the moon and stars with serenades by the surf. Such settings encouraged our love and gave me a different lens for experiencing my island home. And of course there was Magic Island.

No matter how late I came home, my father always was awake and waiting. As soon as the car pulled into the driveway, the outside lights came on. If we sat and talked and kissed too long, my father stepped out the back door. We said our quick goodnights. I reluctantly dashed into the house while he drove away. When Rick's orders sent him to Okinawa, we were relieved he wasn't going into combat, although we knew his orders could change at any time. My parents were relieved too, for other reasons.

We were committed to each other. But being in love is never the end of a story.

Chapter 9:
Dreams of a Married Woman

When the body is finally listened to, it becomes eloquent.
It's like changing a fiddle into a Stradivarius.
—Marian Woodman

The sun, moon, and stars were not in the sky. The cosmos both expanded and contracted inside me. Fiery orb blasting heat and light with the power of life and death. Dull matter lit up by reflected light. Bits of light twinkling in the darkness. The fire and heat of passion reshaped me.

I had defied my father by continuing to see Rick. Then I defied him again. As my interest and concentration in school waned more than waxed, I decided to quit school and work full-time when I was offered a cashier's job in a fashion boutique at Ala Moana Center. No one in my family was really looking out for my happiness; it was all up to me. I convinced myself I would save my earnings to fund my college education on the mainland, to fulfill this dream and finally get away.

For Dad, a college education for all his children was a priority. He wanted this for us because he never had the chance to attend college. Being the eldest child and son, he was groomed for taking over the Chinatown store. The needs of his family and unquestioned obedience to his father were his paramount duties. He didn't have to entreat or persuade us. He assumed we would go since he paved the way by sending us to college-prep schools. Because he had different, more generous, rules for his sons, this did not strike him as being inconsistent or unfair. I dropped out of college in my sophomore year. My siblings completed their bachelor's degrees; two earned master's, and one a doctorate. I was the maverick, the drop-out.

Instead, I opted for love, which I believed was forever. I was confident the intimacy Rick and I shared would inexorably lead to marriage. With this foregone conclusion, what could be more natural than consummating our love? When Rick got orders to ship out, he arranged for a hotel room in Waikīkī, but we didn't stay the whole night. As brazen as I was, I went home to my own bed, and he went back to his barracks.

Honestly, making out was more exciting than making love. Of course, we were still inexperienced and didn't know about female orgasms so, while he climaxed, I felt pleasure mixed with discomfort and some pain. I also had a cold and was medicated, which numbed my experience.

Fortunately for me, Rick believed love was forever too. Before dating him, I never felt so special to anyone or so attractive. Growing up in a large family made me part of a crowd. No one had given me such attention, such affection; surely this was the quality of love that ensured a lifetime together. While my friends shared my happiness, I didn't expect any support from my family. They were completely bewildered by me. My decisions fell below their expectations—a colossal disappointment. They threw up their hands, or more accurately, washed their hands of me. They knew I would do what I wanted and that a sense of family obligation was not strong enough to control my actions. They were right. I was taking charge of my life. My destiny, my mistakes were now in my hands. Of course, I wanted their support. However, I knew without a doubt it was not available; I shouldn't expect it.

I was not entirely ungrateful. I realized my parents had given me a life of comfort and some privilege, gender issues notwithstanding. However, emotionally I was alone and had always felt so. This alienation between teenagers and parents is not uncommon; perhaps it's even necessary to motivate offspring to become independent and separate from their parents, painful as it is for all concerned. And now, true love had entered my life and would carry me away into a shared life where love reigned, where my emotional needs would be understood, where I would not ever feel alone again. Such dreams.

~~~

For a year and a half, our love letters flew across the Pacific while Rick was stationed in Okinawa—blue aerograms or special stationery scented with my perfumes (musk oil) and covered with lipstick kisses. When I wasn't working, I poured out my emotions to Rick in letters. He longed for me as much as I missed him. Fortunately, I had a great job in fashion retailing at Villa Roma: I was promoted to creative director of advertising and promotions. I wore trendy clothes and shoes; I worked with fashion models, photographers, hairstylists, and media people. I read all the fashion rags and did some of the buying. I wrote scripts for fashion shows, ad copy, and a weekly fashion column signed by the manager that our customers eagerly anticipated every Sunday. We had a huge readership; sometimes customers would mob the store when we announced a new shipment of a popular item. Local celebrities relied on us for something glitzy or classic, which of course we reported in the Sunday column. The store became Honolulu's must-go fashion boutique. My work was fulfilling and distracted me from the agony of separation.

Meanwhile, Rick had his job, life on base in a barracks full of homesick guys, who I imagined could easily get into trouble if only for something to do, whether that something was drugs, alcohol, or brothels. I hoped my constant letters would keep Rick safely away from such temptations.

His love letters weren't poetic nor did he write pages and pages like I did, but these were my first love letters. Each one gave me such joy knowing he was thinking of me, missing me. When he sent me a parcel, I excitedly discovered a set of Noritake china for me, for *us* and our future *together!*

When he was discharged in San Diego, he sent me a ring. We knew we wanted to be together although I don't remember that he formally proposed to me. No matter, the ring spoke for his intentions. A few months later in January 1971, I quit my job with immense optimism about our future and flew to join him. Finally, we would be together without the shadow of my parents' disapproval.

He was taking a course in computer operations while we planned a June wedding. It was a small outdoor wedding and reception at one of the hotels in Mission Bay. I beamed in happiness in my long linen dress by Jessica McClintock, a popular designer of ready-to-wear dresses—a Renaissance style, something that Juliet might have worn. And my Romeo wore a light-colored pin-striped suit; his hair was no longer military-cropped, but hung over the top of his ears, and he had a mustache and wore wire-rimmed glasses—the look of the Beatles on their Abbey Road album cover. All of his family attended. A few of my siblings came. I was quietly hoping one of my parents would come even though they had extensive travel plans that summer. Instead, they sent a card and a check. My disappointment erased any memory of whether they had written a personal message.

~~~

The second year into the marriage, we were living in San Francisco on Powell Street, within walking distance to Ghirardelli Square. I was welcomed into the city by friends and the familiarity of a more cosmopolitan population similar to Hawai'i with its racially-mixed families. The city had great restaurants, including Asian food, which I discovered I really missed. I worked as a bank teller, then in retail sales at a shop on Union Square. I loved San Francisco and our spacious apartment with its bay window. When newly-wed life became ordinary, being homesick for Hawai'i and my life there surfaced. The job was so-so, nothing exciting, nothing with real potential. I wanted meaningful work, something to match my ambitions. Love wasn't all I needed after all.

Marriage is never the end of a story. Husbands and wives don't always live happily ever after. At least, not statistically. Marriage is often a goal of romantic, idealistic women like myself, who have no experience living with a partner, much less dealing with family issues that usually come with cohabitation and marriage. I didn't know that maintaining love in a relationship does not happen automatically. I felt disillusioned. Real life, our living together, was far more complicated than the love songs I'd listened to.

~~~

The things we give up for love (or *think* we have to give up for what we *presume* is love), the things we think we have to give up to keep someone else happy—are these personal sacrifices or merely foolish choices? Like giving up my job in Honolulu to be with Rick in San Diego. I knew I would find some kind of work. I had been lucky in getting jobs in the past; I'd never seriously hunted for a job before, certainly not in a strange city. I was young and impetuous and so eager to leave home, ready to flee the nest and test my wings. And I had no doubt that I was ready for marriage. No doubt at all. When we were still struggling and living in San Francisco, my homesickness could no longer be dismissed, so I returned to Honolulu for a visit while Rick continued applying for computer operator jobs. My former boss was opening new stores and I was able to work for her during my stay.

Returning to the islands lifted my spirits enormously. It was so comforting and comfortable to be among friends and family, whom I hadn't seen in almost two years, and to be working with people I'd known for years. I missed Rick, but I was not anxious to return to face uncertainty in the job market. I wanted to work. We both wanted to work. For now, we were working in two different cities. He landed a job as a computer operator for Bank of America while I was in Honolulu. It was a great opportunity for him and he was happy to be in a new career with a reputable company. We spoke by phone.

"When are you planning to come back?"

I didn't know what to say, but he deserved an answer.

"I'm not sure. I've been offered a permanent job here to manage the store, and I'm trying to decide what to do."

Silence. He didn't like this answer.

"I'm happy here and we're really busy! I'd like...."

"Loreen, you've already been gone for a couple of months!"

"I know this is longer than we talked about...."

I had already extended my stay once. I was back in my comfort zone and reluctant to leave it again for the unknown. Was I doubting him? Was I already doubting the marriage? Neither of us wanted to discuss these possibilities. It was the holiday season and an awful time for anyone to be alone.

"...it's just so busy here. I can't leave yet. I just can't." Admittedly, I was enjoying myself surrounded by the people and things that brought me such personal and professional satisfaction. I knew he might be miserable alone in chilly San Francisco where he didn't know many people. He tended to be shy and friendships took time. I knew I should have been more loyal to him; he was my husband after all. It's also true that this was the busy season, which would determine the fate of this new store.

"I haven't accepted the position yet, but can we think about it? Please?"

He could not say no to me.

~~~

We could have made other choices. We could have initiated more honest dialogue about what each of us wanted. I'm not sure we knew how to do this, if we could have even articulated our deepest feelings. Or if we even knew what those feelings were. In the new year, he left his job, packed up our few belongings, and crossed the ocean to join me in Honolulu.

When we moved into a two-bedroom apartment, I realized I'd never had my very own room. I informed Rick I wanted the extra bedroom for my personal use. He didn't object. Neither of us realized the enormity of this decision. Without a specific plan, I moved my clothes into the extra closet, kept a bookshelf for my books, and had a table for craft projects. We still shared a bedroom, but it felt good to have a room for myself, my own private space.

After settling into the apartment, I started having strange dreams. At first they were only fragments of dreams, over and over, again and again. Why was I dreaming about my father's masseur? What was he doing to me? I awakened feeling very disturbed. What did this mean? Puzzlement became certainty: This was not a dream, not something from my imagination. I was remembering what happened to *me*. The events in my dreams had really happened.

The recognition melted over me like warm syrup, dripping over me from head to toes. Disgusting and sticky, it gave me a new skin, a new discomforting lens to see the world. I wanted to shake free from it, to forget these memories. I remained in shock for a long time. I bounced back and forth between doubt and confusion.

I didn't know what to do. If there was anything to do. This knowledge, this recognition of a piece of my life was not inconsequential. A portal to a hidden past had opened. Why were they being revealed now? Had conjugal activities triggered them? Did my now-intimate knowledge of my body unlock a hidden chamber where these secrets lay? Did the truth seep out of my pores and into my dreams? And what other memories might be hiding there?

I held these memories. I acknowledged them as events in my past without knowing what to do with them. I didn't dwell on them, but they came to mind unbidden from time to time, seemingly to inquire: Are you ready to deal with them now? However, I could not conjure any resolution for my past.

Do I tell someone? Whom should I tell? What might they say or do? Would they believe me? Would they believe I only recently remembered this? It seemed risky, very risky.

I don't remember if I told my husband. If I told anyone. I don't think I did. I was not ready to say these words: "I was sexually molested. I was raped when I was ten years old."

Chapter 10:
Terra Incognita

Your vision will become clear only when you look into
your own heart. Who looks outside, dreams; who looks inside, awakes.
—Carl Jung

I love the ocean. Vast, wondrous, mysterious, and on my island of Oʻahu, ever-present. Beyond the ocean, always a horizon. Horizons where sea and sky touch. As a young woman, I found it impossible to not look out and wonder: *What cities and lands and adventures await me there?*

I had no idea how far I might have to travel to find out. It didn't matter. The mystery, the sense of the unknown—these drew me to peer and ponder. To squint my eyes to catch a vision of something beyond my small life.

Something *was* out there. I was dead-certain.

Only several hundred years ago, Europeans believed the world was flat and the horizon marked the end of the world. They predicted that any ship sailing out toward the horizon would plummet off the edge, bringing certain death. To further deter adventure seekers, fearsome and fantastic monsters supposedly lived there at the end of the world. Had anyone actually witnessed such events and survived to tell these tales? No, of course not. Horizons had titillated the imagination until explorers like Ferdinand Magellan, Vasco da Gama, and Christopher Columbus ventured out beyond the horizon and discovered a more fantastic truth.

Horizons offer magic and possibilities. They create the frame for glorious sunsets. Passionate variations of reds, pinks, purples, oranges, golds in broad strokes light the sky and stir my soul. A painting that changes with the light as the sun sinks lower and lower toward the horizon, then falls below it. Twilight, followed by darkness. What's visible: only the night sky pierced by stars and a luminous moon.

And the only sound: my breath releasing in a deep sigh.

~~~

I was awakening to an age of discovery. However, my exploration required me to examine what lay inside of me, not in the external world. Five years into my marriage and feeling settled in Honolulu, I didn't know who I was. The emergence of my secret trauma crystallized this not knowing and raised all kinds of doubt and new questions.

What do you do when you're not who you think you are? So many questions buzzed and buzzed in my head. I could not ignore them. Nor could I answer them although I thought I should. *What did I really want in life? In a loving relationship? In a job or career? How would I sort all this out? How could I find the answers? Find myself?*

Still, I was functional and productive in my daily life; I thought everything was fine, until one day in 1976. A nagging restlessness arose and continued for weeks. Something was wrong, but what? I couldn't shake this feeling. There were no obvious problems to address. A gloomy night descended inside me with no sign of dawn. My employer had expanded from the main store in the Ala Moana Shopping Center to three more: one in Waikīkī and two in Hawai'i Kai; I shuttled back and forth between two of them, working long hours and feeling the stress. Cranky and tired became constant companions. I focused on remedying my work schedule, thinking this would settle my anxiety. But no, I was still agitated and kept asking myself, *What's wrong?*

The answer jumped out like a jack-in-the-box. Aha! My marriage—I was unhappy in my marriage.

Of course. Such a damn fool! How could I commit to a life with someone else when I didn't know who I was or what I wanted? I had married too young. True, I had the body of a woman, but no awareness of myself and my future goals. I had not married Rick; I had married the ideals of being in love, of being married, of being loved and feeling special to someone. The spell was now broken. The illusion fell away. The mist lifted. The flaws in my decisions and all the romantic falsehoods I had once trusted loomed large. Rick dropped into my life when I needed someone to validate me, to be an ally. It could just as well have been Bob or Bill or Jim—any other Marine or any other guy. We were both lovely people, but also lonely, immature, clueless, and inexperienced in the world. We clung to each other with a sense of false belonging, safety, and security. Love was present although our motivations were much more complicated. We both agreed that love leads to marriage; love and marriage seemed reasonable goals. So, we got married.

The truth rose up and punched me. Unmercifully. Marrying Rick had been an act of rebellion against my parents. Marriage created a way out for me: I could finally leave home. I had married under false pretenses. My own pretensions of certainty and maturity boomeranged and crashed into my gut.

Rick represented safety and protection. My ten-year-old-self needed someone to depend on because her parents had failed to keep her safe, and the walls of her home were insufficient for keeping out bad people. My teen-self yearned to be an adult, to take control of her life and be free from other people's authority. And as a woman, I needed safety and protection in order to discover who I was. And indeed, I did feel safe enough to start thinking differently. To pay attention to the questions swirling inside me, including those about my marriage.

Ironically, Dad had been so worried about my safety, that is, my virginity, when I dated Rick. Dad didn't know the damage had already occurred years ago in the family home. Although technically I was a virgin when I met Rick, I had been raped.

Although Rick and I talked, deep communication didn't happen. It wasn't avoidance, it was a lack of experience. Living with my father had not provided learning opportunities for open and honest communications. As a couple, we didn't know how to share our innermost thoughts and feelings. I became increasingly frustrated as the differences in our backgrounds and education created walls.

For example, we both liked movies, but he didn't understand foreign films. The movies *Jaws* or *The Godfather* were enjoyable, but he resisted movies with subtitles. I admit I didn't always understand foreign films either, but I enjoyed having different cinematic experiences and being exposed to foreign cultures and ideas. Growing up hearing multiple languages, I liked the sounds of languages other than my own. My ears enjoyed the various tones, rhythms, pitches. Also, foreign films forced me to think more deeply than American films, to consider life through different lenses. Art and literature offered me intellectual stimulation. Rick, on the other hand, was more comfortable in a concrete world. Tools and wood, building something. Biking or swimming, interacting in nature. Fixing a car or explaining the mechanics of a car. I was discovering a craving for interactions with people interested in ideas, philosophy, aesthetics, not only the mundane events and problems of the day.

I started journaling. I had never done this before. What prompted me to face the blank page and start scrawling? I guess there was so much churning inside me pushing and demanding expression. Talking with my family or to Rick didn't seem viable options. I wasn't sure how to even put these feelings into speech. The safest place was on the page where no response was expected. I bought a simple nondescript notebook, went into my room and closed the door. I was alone in my own private space. I picked up an ordinary pen. Where should I start? What should I write? I hoped to be profound and brilliant. Instead, the words flowed, but were barely coherent—pages and pages of rambling and more rambling. Basically, this writing was me talking to myself, to hear what was inside, what was in my heart, what I feared, what I couldn't articulate. All my hidden thoughts. I needed to open all the doors, give myself permission to walk through and look around. Be willing to see what was there.

The words were not as important as the act of writing. Perhaps no one else would understand this writing or that this was a radical act—claiming something deeply felt for myself. It was very emotional with tears often spilling onto the page. Tears of relief and gladness. Also grief. Of having felt lost for so long. Living to please others had required burying my own needs. Yet, I knew this sacrificial behavior was wrong even as I went through the motions. Perhaps I had strong-willed, strong-minded female ancestors guiding me. Perhaps I'd lived a previous lifetime as a man with a sense of entitlement that carried forward into this lifetime. Perhaps my soul had an intimate knowledge of American individualism that rallied to this act of self-expression.

Wanting my own room in our first Honolulu apartment, my own private space, had been an initiation. In this room I permitted my heart and mind to open. Journaling was both action and response. The tears kept coming as the pen moved across the page. It didn't matter if the words made no sense, if it was gibberish conveying inner confusion and chaos. It was my soul breaking free. It didn't need to be pretty. It was for me and no one else.

As the writing shifted into a practice of self-reflection, the clutter began to clear away to glimmers of insight and deeper understanding. I was probing my own mind and heart. I was discovering myself through tears and ink. Sometimes I went to a park to write. I sat on the ground under the spreading branches of a monkey pod tree, which shaded me in warmth and safety. I let myself be with the waves of both words and tears. I was learning the power of writing. To write with abandon, for pure pleasure and not anyone's approval. This writing, this process of writing, belonged to me entirely. For me. About me. By my own hand. I was okay. I was going to be okay. I was not going crazy.

Here's what was crazy-making: For whatever reason I believed I had to remain fixed, to remain the person whom Rick fell in love with. If I changed, it would threaten the marriage. If I didn't, I was condemning myself to being stuck at 18 years old—truly a bad idea. I'm not sure where this notion came from, but it was embedded in my unconscious mind, and I molded myself accordingly during my married years. But I knew I couldn't remain frozen in time. Change was necessary.

I still wanted to complete a college degree at some point; I wanted to learn, grow, and improve myself. In other words, I wanted my life to include more than the status quo, more than work and marriage. I felt light-headed and anxious when I wrote this in my journal—capturing these amorphous ideas into words on the page, something tangible. It seemed heretical to want a life beyond marriage, but I was getting more and more clear that a traditional life in which the husband has control and the wife is subservient was not for me. I had felt so confident that marriage would be all-encompassing, would satisfy my every need. The real risk lay in having my own mind. Would my pursuit of a college degree threaten the marriage? Was I supposed to give up college *again*?

More questions. My seeking led to more questions: What decisions would I make about my life if I were single? I dared to wonder: *What if I didn't have a spouse?*

I had never lived alone or completely supported myself. Could I do it? It wouldn't be easy, and it forced me to assess my job, to consider my life in terms beyond the immediate future. Did I want to continue working in fashion retailing? Was I getting paid enough for all the work I was doing, all the long hours? Was it enough to support myself? What about retirement or profit-sharing? I had worked for this company for nearly ten years already— did I have a future there with financial and professional growth? These were questions no one could help me with. I had to face them directly, figure things out, make decisions to take care of myself. Taking these steps would be crucial. Crippled by childhood memories of asking for money did not make this easy.

~~~

When Rick arrived in Honolulu, computer operator jobs were nonexistent. He adapted and soon found a job as a cabinetmaker—a union job with a well-established local company that paid well. Still, it was a major adjustment to go from his white-collar job in San Francisco to a blue-collar job in Honolulu.

His biggest challenge was being haole in a shop filled with local guys; these brown- and yellow-skinned bruddahs spoke Pidgin, not good kine mainland English. He not only looked different, he did not understand the local lingo. He wasn't used to being a minority, and he got picked on and harassed. I think most of it was harmless, but then again, maybe not, at least not from his point of view. I was sympathetic. I had felt marginalized in San Diego, but I knew Rick was a decent guy and a hard worker. I hoped the situation would improve with time.

Living and working in Honolulu was entirely different from being in the Marines, which had insulated Rick from the everyday reality of island living. In this artificial cocoon, he hadn't felt like a minority because he lived on base where everyone pretty much looked like him. Military life was highly structured and dominated by white males. Now he was a civilian and immersed in island culture, which mostly welcomed and accepted him—meaning my family and friends received him without judgment into our circle. However, his work environment threw him way out of his comfort zone. I was thriving in my job, while he dreaded interactions with co-workers very different from himself, in both appearance and social background. Although genuinely likable, he felt outnumbered by the bruddahs and alienated. His complaints became frequent, but we couldn't talk about it. We didn't know how.

Cultivating friends and talking to strangers did not come naturally to Rick, so our social events centered around people I knew. That was fine in the beginning when it was fun to introduce everyone to "my husband." After a few years, I began feeling annoyed by his dependence on me and hoped he would develop his own circle of friends. I needed girl-time with my friends. Didn't he need guy-time? So far, he had no buddies and couldn't relate to his co-workers.

Life is full of ironies. When we were single, we wanted to be together all the time. Just the two of us were more than enough. Once we were married, we were always together and I needed space for other people in my life.

The good news was that my parents and Rick got along. Their defenses came down when we were married and living in Honolulu. They got to know him and saw that he treated me well and was respectful to them; they recognized he was a good guy, even an asset to the family. My parents had rental property, and Rick had great handyman skills and could build things—skills my brothers lacked. Employed as a cabinetmaker, he had access to all kinds of building supplies. My father was ultimately a practical person; Rick's usefulness and the future possibility of grandchildren softened his stance. My parents believed babies were inevitable for married people, so they wanted to be on good terms with us. But Rick and I weren't ready for children. We were busy working. Rick worked with his hands, and I worked in a creative, collaborative environment to sell affordable styles laced with the latest fashion gossip and glamor. We lived simply and fell into a routine.

Rick often sat at home after work. He could have gone out when I was working late. Instead he found a friend in paka lōlō, or pot, which he had begun smoking in the service. He masked his loneliness and unhappiness with weed as I began questioning the marriage more and more—questioning myself. *Who am I? Should I stay with Rick? Or would this impede my self-discovery?*

Rick and I *were* very different. I had overlooked the obvious when we were dating. Race, class, and education could no longer be ignored. Background and upbringing contribute so much to a person's sense of the world and one's place in it. His view was not wrong, only different from mine, which I thought would not change. I enjoyed and thrived on a full buffet of diverse cultures. Variety and different seasonings were normal to me. As newlyweds on a budget, we ate a lot of Hamburger Helper. He was happy with that—hamburgers, potatoes, with lots of ketchup were fine anytime. When I made stir-fry one evening and saw him put butter on his rice, I had to hide my disgust and look away.

I wanted love in my life, but also needed freedom to be me—whoever I turned out to be. I was confused and scared. Still, my imagination began considering new possibilities. My journaling fueled a desire to write more, perhaps take writing classes. Acknowledging this made me recall my love for music and art. Maybe I could take singing lessons. Drawing and reading had occupied much of my childhood. I wanted time to read more, pursue these interests, and someday complete my college degree. So much had fallen away that I wanted to reclaim.

I wondered what Rick wanted, other than a different job, or if he had ever asked himself this. I didn't know if he wanted to grow in new directions. *Did he resent having to leave San Francisco and his job? Did he blame me for this?* When he was high, he was in no condition to have anything resembling a real conversation. I often came home after closing the store at 9 p.m. and found him lolling on the carpeted floor in the living room with a joint. I felt powerless and frustrated. Smoking weed would not resolve anything. I knew he had worked hard that day too and deserved some leisure time, but he was smoking too much, too often. It was creating distance between us. That he preferred to escape somewhere into a cloud far away from reality rather than deal with our problems underscored how differently we approached life's challenges. At the same time, we were both avoiding any confrontation. I also was escaping—into the demands of my job. Our world together was crumbling as we began existing more and more in two separate realities.

No one in either of our families had been divorced. Marriage, good or bad, was for life. I wanted this to be true, but what did we know about spending a lifetime together? How did people do this? How did they sustain a marriage over the years and decades? I could not fathom another year of this, much less decades.

Once again I was about to shake off caution, break new ground, and probably upset my family. I had been so confident about getting married. Now I needed to take responsibility for this mistake.

~~~

It is hereby ordered, adjudged and decreed that a decree of absolute divorce is hereby granted to Plaintiff, the bonds of matrimony between Plaintiff and Defendant are hereby dissolved....

Within twelve months I was divorced, living alone, and supporting myself for the first time. Even with a new, better-paying job, I lived in fear and uncertainty about where I would land. I was riding a whirlwind. All I could do was hold on. Just hold on and keep facing forward.

When I received the divorce decree, I looked at the envelope with my lawyer's name on it. We had gone to a hearing at Family Court in early September on a date near my parents' wedding anniversary. A couple of weeks later the decree arrived in the mail. I thought, "This is it!" I took a deep breath and opened the envelope. Reading the sobering words, I suddenly had to sit down. Each word felt heavy, as if attached to a boulder. This piece of paper, this legal document officially ended seven years of marriage, a total of ten years of my life with Rick. I didn't expect to feel so...so somber, so overwhelmed by its finality. It's what I wanted, right? I wanted a different life,

I wanted to be single, so here it was. In 1977, I was 28 and on my own to face the world.

Tears slid down my cheeks. This was confirmation that my marriage had failed—a very personal failure and one more for the statistics. Unlike weddings, which are celebrations with family and friends, divorce is a very private moment, an empty affair.

Months ago, when we announced to my parents that we were getting a divorce, they were visibly upset. On Dad's advice we agreed to separate for six months before proceeding. Everyone hoped that time would alter our decision, but I knew I would not change my mind. I wanted to think that Rick and I had mutually agreed to the divorce, but it had been my decision. At the time, I saw no other option. Rick could have continued in this hapless marriage, though he seemed unhappy to me. Did he know he was unhappy? Had he admitted this to himself? We were leaning on each other in various ways instead of supporting each other to be strong individuals. I didn't have my driver's license and Rick drove us everywhere or I arranged rides with friends. During our separation, I was determined to change this. Rick taught me to drive. I acquired a driver's license and purchased my first car: a new Datsun.

In marriage, we had two incomes, which blinded me from seeing that I was underpaid. I was making nearly the same salary as four years ago. Friendship with the manager turned out to be a liability instead of a benefit; my employer of nearly ten years could not, would not offer an increase in salary or benefits. It was a small family-owned business that had grown from one store to four during my tenure, and I took pride in having played some part in its success. Well, it was time for a change. It would have been simpler to stay in the job after my divorce, but life wasn't so simple any more. With equal parts of sadness and excitement, I looked for another job and found one with a media consulting firm.

I was facing a new horizon. The world I knew was disappearing. Pieces of myself were falling away—big chunks. I wasn't sure whether I was unraveling or coming together. On the edge of disaster or transforming, a phoenix rising from the fire. What in the world would become of me?

Chapter 11:
In My Own Skin

I take pleasure in my transformations. I look quiet and
consistent, but few know how many women are in me.
— Anaïs Nin

In junior high when we were assigned to research and write a paper on one of the major organ systems in the body, most students selected the circulatory, nervous, digestive, reproductive, or cardiovascular systems. I chose something less obvious: the skin, the outer layer of the human body that interacts with the world around us that differentiates us from everyone else. It holds together our internal organs in a complex structure with other essentials like tissues, muscles, bones, and blood to function in a grand scheme that scientists still don't completely understand. The largest organ in the human body, skin is essential, yet its importance often goes unrecognized. Comprised of epidermis, dermis, and subcutaneous fat, it's a thin layer that shields us from environmental elements, harmful bacteria, other people. The skin is responsive, sensitive, and intelligent; hundreds of nerve endings per square inch constantly process what surrounds us, whether animate or inanimate. Looking back, I believe I chose to study the skin because of my unconscious desire for human touch: a pat on the shoulder, a caress on the cheek, a hug, an arm entwined with another's arm, leaning into another body—touching that means someone cares. I wanted this physical contact, skin touching skin, to confirm I am seen and not invisible. I am seen and I am loved.

Sexual pleasure offered me a new way of touching and being touched. As a newly divorced woman, I was unsure of myself, doubting my attraction to men. I didn't know any divorced young women who might advise me in navigating through these uncharted waters. Suddenly, good-looking men started chatting with me in stores and on the bus. I wasn't doing anything unusual. I don't think I looked differently or acted differently. Except I *was* different. I began looking more at men than I had when married—casually looking, but definitely noticing, appraising with an appreciative eye. Was I friendlier? Was I obviously single? I was surprised that meeting men came so easily.

~~~

"Let's say you like apples. It's the only fruit you know. You like how it looks, its crunchy texture, its fragrance, the way it tastes, and the juices released when you're chewing the pulp. It's satisfying and you're happy eating this fruit. You think you will never tire of it. But you haven't tasted any other fruit, and many kinds are available out there. You might like something better." Shelley said this with a knowing look, insinuating she wasn't talking about fruit.

Shelley was a successful sales rep in Los Angeles, who became a good friend of my boss, Marsha, the general manager and buyer at Villa Roma. One of the first Jewish people I met, she was a savvy salesperson with several popular lines of clothing. We met on one of our buying trips. She wasn't very tall, but had a luscious, curvy body and looked gorgeous with her makeup, hair, and clothing arranged to perfection. She was in the rag business and embraced all that was necessary to looking the part. Several years older than me, Marsha was married with four children. Shelley was a career woman and knew the fashion business. On earlier trips, she had taken Marsha under her wing, sharing her expertise, introducing her around the fashion mart, taking her to trendy restaurants and points of interest in sprawling L.A. Friendship developed between these two women, strengthened with each of Marsha's seasonal trips. Shelley was outspoken and direct, with no topic too sensitive to discuss. She knew Marsha had married her first love and that I was planning to marry mine.

We were at Shelley's condo in the Marina Del Rey relaxing after a long day and talking about love and marriage. She asked us, "If you've slept with only one man, how do you know what you like? Really like?"

It was a fair question. However, since I was in love for the first time and believed in one and only love, she could have been speaking Swahili or ancient Greek. I could not hear or understand her words. A few years into the marriage, these words came back to me in 3-D. I now understood. My marriage with its familiar routine, including routine sex, had lost its shiny newness like a balloon losing its helium. How did I know what I wanted? How did I presume to know anything about love? Sex? Marriage?

However, Shelley's words weren't really about men. They were about me and my self-esteem, or lack thereof.

At Villa Roma, I worked alongside gorgeous, young women—tall, lissome, seemingly confident. Many local girls worked part-time and juggled work, school, and sorority commitments. All salesgirls were encouraged to purchase the store's clothing and accessories at a discount, to model the merchandise on the sales floor. Some also modeled when the store presented full-scale fashion shows. This was a world of beautiful women. Since I did not include myself in this category, I merely hoped to blend in.

I didn't believe I was hot and desirable like other young women. I never saw myself as pretty. I tanned darker than my siblings and my brothers used to tease me. As a child, I liked tagging along when my brothers were going somewhere with the other older kids from the neighborhood. I would follow them. Most times they didn't want me to come. Clyde or Ben turned around and said, "Stop following us. Go home and play with your dolls." But I kept following them. They turned around again, and one of them said, "You can't come. You're too dark. You look like a niggah." They laughed and ran off. My feet stayed stuck to the ground. Their meanness came through even though I didn't know what a niggah was. Forget them, I thought. Obviously, my fair-skinned sisters were pretty. At some point as a teenager, I concluded I would never be a beauty, but I could maintain lovely skin, youthful and glowing. I headed to the cosmetics counter at Liberty House, a local department store, and invested in a skin-care regimen for my face: cleanser, toner, moisturizer.

At work, I overheard the salesgirls chattering about their dates, boyfriends, flirtations, and innuendoes. I witnessed the parade of men who came into the store to see them. Some of these young women had multiple boyfriends all vying for their affections. Some were serial monogamists with a new beau every few months. They were young and having fun, definitely not ready to be serious about anyone yet.

Fashion is a seductive business. Who doesn't want to be pretty, to look stylish and be attractive? As a child, I played with my mother's clothing and makeup. For girls, such socialization starts early.

Playing with my sisters as children, we made up a game. The three of us crowded together over a magazine. The goal was selecting the prettiest woman or girl on the page and being the first to touch her picture and declare,

"That's me!" When someone turned the page, shouts of "That's me! That's me!" would break out while little fingers darted over the open pages. Then the next page and the next, until the very last page was done. It didn't matter if it was a storybook, a comic book, or a magazine like *Life* or *McCall's*. We longed to be pretty like the women we saw in the photographs, illustrations, and advertisements. We longed to be pretty like movie stars, Wonder Woman, and Breck Shampoo models.

As a teenager, even though I wore shapeless, unflattering uniforms—a white middy blouse with black tie and dark pleated skirt—and clunky oxford shoes, I paid attention to my hair, checked out blushes and lipsticks, noticed if my skin was breaking out, and purchased contact lenses the first summer I earned enough money to buy them.

Landing in fashion retailing at nineteen threw me into a new world full of glitz and glamor. I adapted quickly because it was such fun. Imagine, repackaging myself with the latest new styles; it was make-over heaven. Because my family raised me in practical ways, I never dreamed of having a fashion wardrobe. Besides wearing the same uniform for eight years, my other clothing were hand-me-downs. The economics of a large family prohibited the expense of new clothing for everyone. Rarely did I get something new or go shopping for clothes. I took sewing classes for a couple of summers and made a few things, but these dresses never had the finished look of something store-bought. At Villa Roma, I saw the newest fashions arrive and could grab something I liked before it hit the sales floor. I enjoyed wearing the latest fashions and learning to accessorize with scarves and jewelry, working with different fabrics like challis and moire, colors like aubergine and cranberry, and patterns like paisley, tie-dyes, granny prints; and collaborating with an array of creative professionals—designers, graphic artists, display artists, advertising professionals. My imagination flourished as I managed the store's advertising and promotions, which generated customers flocking into the store ready to buy. It was heady stuff for any young woman. I loved my job.

This world focused on the external, what lay on the surface, the image of the moment. The icon might be Twiggy today, then Barbarella or Annie Hall, Farrah Fawcett or Cher. It was ever-changing and required constant vigilance to keep pace, to stay ahead of the competition. Meanwhile, what was I thinking and feeling? What was going on inside of me? No time for considering such matters. On one hand, I was earning a respectable living and felt independent. On the other hand, I was still living at home when I met Rick and didn't know how to drive. I was trapped by tradition: A woman did not leave her parents' home until she married or went away to college. I was living a conflicted life—not the first time nor the last—but I didn't recognize this. I was too distracted to consider what I really wanted to do with my life, to consider my future and the realities of this fashion business, to make time for self-reflection. To be serious about me and my long-term goals. To recognize my low self-esteem. Despite my bravado, my bold decisions, and professional confidence, I was haunted by a secret feeling of worthlessness, a sense of irreparable damage.

As a single woman of twenty-eight, I felt lucky to meet attractive men and fell in love again and again. Most were young and virile. Some were older by ten years or more. Some were great lovers and others, merely okay. A few had the occasional equipment failure; impotence in men not much older than me was a surprise, but being held and caressed was pleasure enough. Some demonstrated creative ways to arouse me. They were interested in my satisfaction, while delaying their own—and enjoyed showing off their sexual prowess. I was fully appreciative. I learned that imagination can definitely compensate for short-comings. Some were married or otherwise involved, professing to be in so-called "open relationships."

I was saying yes often, but I said no to an aging local celebrity and a married politician, both of whom tried to seduce me. Lechery was not appealing. I also said no to men I worked with; in one case, it required super-human will power. He was my boss, a young and gorgeous Brit, who was well-liked and had a good sense of humor. We liked and respected each other; we worked well together in a busy department. We flirted a bit and enjoyed the sparks flying; despite the office gossip, we never slept together. Workplace relationships can be complicated enough without romantic entanglements.

I was seduced by a well-turned physique, a sensitive face, a sense of humor, an affinity for words and higher education, musical or culinary talents, a boyish masculinity, or simple joie de vivre. And of course, sexual chemistry, which I convinced myself was love, launched me into many affairs. I enjoyed tactile intimacy, the sensuality of skin, the numerous ways of touching one another. I wanted touch and love, and sex offered both. Men loved the softness of my skin. Its fine hairs were invisible and I never had to shave my legs. Pleasure ruled and I didn't realize how confused I was. I kept hearing Shelley's words: "There are so many kinds of fruit. You just might like something better." Yes, indeed.

All the same, I admit that love made me stupid. I was blind to men who were troubled, the commitment-phobic, the untrustworthy and inconsiderate, the truly cheap, and others incapable of enduring relationships for whatever reason. I didn't recognize the cads and the dishonesty of those cheating on their wives and girlfriends—their general lack of respect for women and my own complicity. If I had thought about what I was doing, I would have had to confess to my selfish needs and lack of self-esteem.

This period of time in the late 1970s and into the 1980s provided learning and youthful indulgence for me and many others in a carefree period following an unpopular war (Vietnam) and an unpopular president (Nixon), both damaging to the national psyche. The women's liberation movement informed my sense of independence, fueled my desire for freedom over my body and my life. I was keen to see if I could make it on my own, to confirm that I could have a different life than my mother's. Birth control pills accelerated this freedom. It was an intoxicating time to be a woman, reinforced by songs like *I Am Woman* ("I am strong, I am invincible, I am woman."), while television shows like *The Mary Tyler Moore Show* and *Charlie's Angels* featured independent, strong working women. Women were also leading governments, such as Indira Gandhi in India, Golda Meir in Israel, and Margaret Thatcher in the United Kingdom. I was reading books like Gail Sheehy's *Passages*, Erica Jong's *Fear of Flying*, and Marilyn French's *The Women's Room*. Life ahead held much promise.

I was also aware in the 1970s that a renaissance in Hawaiian culture was gaining momentum. Young Hawaiians were embracing many aspects of their culture, some formerly banned by law, such as hula and the Hawaiian language, and exhibiting a new pride in being Hawaiian. A young generation of Hawaiian and local musicians began composing, performing, and attracting crowds: Peter Moon, Robert and Roland Cazimero, Keola and Kapono Beamer, Jerry Santos, Cecilio and Kapono, and others. Playing slack-key guitar, or Hawaiian-style tunings, ignited a younger generation of Hawaiian musicians. Both men and women enrolled in hula schools to learn ancient and contemporary styles of dancing so that hula hālau, or schools, proliferated on all the islands. Hawaiian language could now be spoken and taught. As a result, Hawaiian-language immersion schools and Hawaiian studies classes were established to ensure the continuation of this cultural knowledge for future generations.

Cultural pride intensified when a replica of an ancient double-hulled voyaging canoe named *Hōkūleʻa* was built in Hawaiʻi and successfully sailed from Tahiti to Hawaiʻi in 1976 without using modern instruments or charts. The Polynesian navigational system observes celestial bodies (stars, moon, sun), wind, and waves; *Hōkūleʻa*'s voyage confirmed this ancient wisdom, specifically the migration and seaworthy skills of Hawaiian ancestors, who arrived on these islands around two thousand years ago. It was a new dawn for Hawaiians.

As I became drawn to this fervor surrounding Hawaiian culture, especially the music and the dancing, I began to understand the layers of meaning in the poetry, songs, and dances, which convey a celebration of nature and often human sexuality. Pele's fire also refers to sexual passion.

~~~

This period during my late twenties was not a time of determined misbehavior. I was definitely breaking out of my good-girl role, but this was not me being a girl gone wild. Young, childless, and single, I was eager to embrace all of life and welcomed new experiences. I plunged into the school of life, ready to learn, to sort out myself and the world around me. Fortunately, I did not require recreational drugs and alcohol, which never appealed to me. I was already high—flying on my own, enjoying this new sexual freedom. However, learning and growing did require self-centeredness, and admittedly I was self-absorbed. Such behavior was definitely not Chinese and I made mistakes along the way. Who didn't? Who doesn't?

Looking back at these years of sexual experimentation makes me wonder. Following years of therapy, I recognize that being raped was not my fault, is not my shame. Still, I wonder if my "skin hunger," this desire to be touched and loved as a child, somehow attracted a sexual predator. Is there such a thing as unconscious messaging? Definitely there are appropriate and inappropriate ways of touching. A child does not have such awareness. As a woman, was I using sexual pleasure to erase the trauma and reclaim my body? Or was I rejecting my body as I took new lovers again and again?

~~~

In this new freedom, I didn't grasp how vulnerable I was. The seduction of sexual desire is one thing. The seduction of ideas about personal transformation is another. I encountered the human potential movement, aka personal growth aka new age spirituality—many groups adopted some form of ancient practices based on Eastern religions and spirituality. In the early 1970s, Bruce Lee popularized martial arts in the U.S. and had a huge following; on television, David Carradine starred in the popular show *Kung Fu*. The Beatles had visited India to study transcendental meditation with their guru and popularized meditation and Eastern philosophies. A new awareness opened up possibilities for those steeped in Western culture and religion.

The 1970s brought opportunities for expanding my consciousness. I attended a popular weekend seminar developed by Werner Erhard; "est" or Erhard Seminar Training claimed to transform peoples' lives. I practiced transcendental meditation. I did talk-therapy before and after the divorce. Friends referred me to psychics and astrologers, so I scheduled a few sessions. All were fascinating new tools for self-awareness, for accessing information about myself.

In 1980, Mount St. Helen's shocked the Pacific Northwest with a historic eruption that ended 123 years of dormancy. This volcano, some 90 miles south of Seattle, expelled a column of ash 80,000 feet into the sky, which fell in 11 states. The blast flattened about 230 acres of forest and sent mudslides as far as the Columbia River, almost 50 miles away. It killed 57 people.

In this same year, I met the Empyrean community of rebirthers, who espoused unconditional love for the self and others. These were new concepts: loving myself first, treating myself as important, the way I wanted others to treat me, not waiting for others to validate and love me; finding the source of love inside me, not outside. My family had definite conditions for being loved and accepted. Marriage required certain constraints as well. Finding myself among people who offered a new way of being, who seemed genuinely loving and caring, who opened their arms readily for warm hugs, and who really listened—well, these were my kind of people.

I signed up for rebirthing sessions—a deep-breathing process that can unlock trauma held in the body. Rebirthers believed people stored trauma in their bodies, including the experience of being born. From a warm, safe, dark, watery environment, the infant is forced into a cold, foreign, brightly lit room. Trauma was familiar, but I had no idea about the unexpressed, hidden feelings in my body. The goal was the release of these deep feelings, often unexpressed sadness and anger, to free up energy, which meant more room for joy and aliveness. Letting go of old emotional pain would allow me to be more fully myself in the present, uncovering the power and beauty we all have inside us.

I was open-minded and willing to see if it worked. If it didn't, I would discontinue the sessions. Simple. I signed up for a few sessions. Talk therapy had helped me in ways I hadn't expected. When my therapist first asked me, "How do you feel about that?" I didn't know what to say. No one had ever asked for my opinion about myself and my life. Slowly, I found my voice and began to verbalize my thoughts and feelings. I was hoping that rebirthing would help me further.

It did. Rebirthing gave me an opportunity to explore deeper, to venture below the surface into my body, to allow suppressed feelings to reach consciousness. And God knows, there were lots of emotions not permitted when I was growing up. The sessions did not involve a lot of talking. It was experiential; the rebirthing breath released whatever I was ready to deal with.

Creating a safe and loving environment, the rebirther welcomed me with a hug. We chatted for a few minutes about current events in my life, about any fear or anxiety I might have about the session. Next, I lay on my back on a daybed and focused on my breathing. She dimmed the light and turned on some relaxing background music, much like in a massage session, sat on a chair next to me, ready with a blanket if needed. She ensured I was breathing deeply into my abdomen. Then out. It was a continuous, circular breath in and out of my core. She reminded me to breathe when I stopped or when I felt pain in my body. "Keep going. You can breathe through this." Every session was different. Sometimes I would see colors or images during a session. Other times, I would feel an intense emotion and start crying. Whether or not the emotion was tied to an event didn't matter. Experiencing the emotion was a form of release. For me and many women, sadness was an acceptable emotion but anger was not. With gentle coaching from the rebirther, I got to feel and express anger during some sessions, to move it out of my body. Anger at my rapist. Anger at my father. I learned to scream, feel the rage rippling through my body, and let the rage explode out of my body in words I never dared utter before: "Fuck you! Fuck you! FUCK YOU!" "How dare you!" My throat became raw as I continued screaming into a pillow. I flailed my arms and body as I screamed. This physicality of emotions was new. The idea that emotions are neither positive nor negative was also new information. It made sense that we need to be okay with a whole range of human emotions, to acknowledge whatever feelings are present, which is not the same thing as acting on our emotions. I might feel violently angry, but I should not act violently.

At the end of a session, after a release, a beatific peace settled over me. The cells in my body hummed serenely, and I was fully conscious of the sensation. In this heightened state, I opened my eyes and saw my surroundings shimmering and renewed, which is how I felt about myself. The rebirther spoke soothing words to validate me and my experience, to affirm my goodness and worthiness. It was remarkable. Powerful. This feeling of being brand-new and open to the goodness the world had to offer, like a newborn child. Writing daily affirmations would help to transform negative and erroneous thoughts about myself that I had embodied.

One evening, after I had experienced a few sessions, I attended a public rebirthing seminar in a hotel ballroom. One of the teachers was speaking on the platform. I raised my hand. When I stood, an uncontrollable emotion swept through me; I opened my mouth and a piercing cry filled the room. It was a primal scream from the bowels of my being, the howling of a wounded animal. It was the cry of pain and rage I did not emit when I was raped. It was the cry I did not emit when my dreams revealed I was raped. Almost twenty years after the trauma, I finally erupted.

I was not told to control myself or to shut up. I was not shamed for making a public spectacle of myself. On the contrary, I was acknowledged. I was congratulated. I was seen and loved. This ugly darkness in me was revealed and I was *still* loved.

This was the acceptance I wanted. This was the safety I was seeking, and over the next two years as a client, then part of IPEP, or Intensive Personal Evolution Program, and later as a rebirther trainee, I worked through layers of anger, sadness, fear, and grief concerning childhood traumas, including the rape. I had not been consciously looking for another family, but I experienced a strong sense of belonging and love here in this spiritual community. I blossomed as a rebirther and seminar leader. I learned to release old pain, rage, grief. Regular bodywork and massage assisted my physical healing. Therapeutic touch provided another layer of safety—touch without any sexual agenda. I also observed physical changes in clients and other students: People sometimes looked younger after letting go of old emotions. Other times, their faces and bodies appeared lighter, not so dense and heavy.

I traveled to San Diego to assist the leaders in workshops. They had connected with the popular and charismatic leader of Terry Cole-Whitaker Ministries. A former Religious Science pastor, The Reverend Terry Cole-Whitaker established her own church and attracted thousands of followers. After experiencing rebirthing, she wanted her staff and congregation to experience this transformative healing process. So, several of us rebirthers flew from Honolulu to assist. Over time, branches of the Honolulu rebirthing community expanded to Vancouver, B.C., San Diego, and Albuquerque, while other unrelated rebirthing communities grew in other parts of the country. Rebirthing was not a household word, but it was spreading. At the same time, other personal transformational programs and entities, such as Scientology, Ramtha, and Money and You, were becoming popular and sometimes controversial. In 1983, I felt ready to move into the expanding world of rebirthing and headed to Vancouver.

I was welcomed into the community and became an active member. I was comfortable there, but questions started to bubble up, and I realized we rebirthers were not special or even elevated in our consciousness, only regular humans striving for self-improvement and self-empowerment. Individuals may have experienced moments of exquisite clarity and loving energy after a rebirthing session, just as I had experienced incredible joy and aliveness in every cell, a sense of well-being and inner peace, and being reborn, made whole again. However, we weren't enlightened yet, not even close.

~~~

Vancouver offered several popular dance clubs. Since rebirthing was often intense work, going out to dance provided an effective means of mitigating some of the intensity. The dance floor was packed, but one man caught my attention with his boyish looks and confidence. *Good dancer. Smooth, very smooth.* Little did I know. He noticed me and asked me to dance.

I love dancing and matched his moves, my long straight waist-length hair whipping around to the rock music. We danced together a couple of times, the chemistry charging the air around us. His name was Roy.

The following week, my friends and I went to a different club. Roy and his friends were there, too. The stars seemingly had aligned for us to meet again. We connected, danced to a few songs, chatted. He bought me a drink. When it was time to leave, he offered to drive me home.

He confessed he was ending a relationship with his girlfriend. He didn't go into detail, only that he was moving out soon. I was already in his thrall, so

I believed him and didn't probe further. When we got to my place, he walked me to the door. As far as I was concerned, the evening was over. Perhaps only a goodnight kiss. The mutual attraction was evident. We started kissing slowly, then passionately until we feverishly fell through the door. Like his dancing, he was an artful lover.

He did get his own place. We continued seeing each other and we fell in love. Many weeks later, he told me he had herpes. Seemingly remorseful, he expressed his fear about disclosing this, and *I* ended up comforting *him*. I should have slapped him in the face. I *wished* I had slapped him and walked away, far away. But I was already in love, and as I've said before, love makes me stupid. Hopelessly in love; hopelessly stupid. I never even considered that he should use a condom, that I could ask him to wear one.

Not surprisingly, I had an outbreak and was diagnosed with this sexually transmitted disease. I thought he was the love of my life and we were going to be together, so it didn't matter. He ardently professed his love for me, even introducing me to his family. Convinced we were serious about each other, I overlooked his dishonesty, how he manipulated me, and the pain of the lesions. This was not the kind of forever I had dreamed about.

We were playful together, laughing often, both in and out of bed. We were good together. Our libidos seemed well matched. Experiencing sexual ecstasy like never before, I felt we became fused into one body, one spirit. We decided to live together. The relationship seemed to be growing in the right direction.

I was still working as a rebirther and was very involved in the community. I had invited him to some events, to participate and be part of this "human potential" work. It was a large part of my life and I felt it was important that he become more familiar with my work. After all, I had visited his workshop where he designed and built furniture.

"You can tell me all about it. Explain it to me."

"Well, it's not something you can understand by talking about it. Rebirthing is experiential. I can describe my experience, but everyone is different. It's very individual. If you come to a seminar, you'll understand what I mean."

He could not be persuaded. Even though many people had benefited, he wasn't interested. He didn't need to explore this deep stuff. I admired his strong sense of self, but I could not dismiss the thought that Roy might be fearful about examining his inner landscape. However, I backed off and let it go.

So often the renegade, I was the only rebirther living with someone outside of the community. Before we found an apartment together, we had been spending weekends together. In truth, it was rather refreshing to be with someone not involved with my work. It was healthier for me. We could talk about other things, hang out with whomever we wanted. And I got genuine breaks from this work that was often all-consuming.

We had been together well over a year when I began to feel restless about continuing to live in Vancouver. I questioned the leadership in the community and my role there. Unconditional love was easy to talk about and difficult to practice. A hierarchy developed when the leaders created a separation from the rest of the community. I began questioning the business practices involved in maintaining a spiritual community; there seemed to be a very thin line between the teachers' business goals and the avowed spiritual practices. We were constantly enrolling people into more seminars, more private and group rebirthing sessions, more rebirthing trainings, and other events. Tithing to the teachers became an oft-repeated message. I noticed what appeared to be a dependency by some devotees on the community and its teachers—a dependency that the teachers encouraged, tacitly and not so tacitly, instead of encouraging independent thinking and personal mastery.

I've never used the word "cult" to refer to my rebirthing community. Perhaps my loyalty blinded me to this possibility. Most of the members were well-intentioned, but the leaders' control over people's lives could have been construed as a form of mind-control. The leaders' self-importance and need for devotees were perhaps unconscious, but still antithetical to the dawning of a new age.

Roy wasn't happy when I began talking about returning to the U.S., but he did nothing to persuade me to stay. Clearly he wasn't ready for more commitment.

I trusted my intuition, which told me to leave Vancouver, the community, and teachers to work independently. I hoped that this rebirthing community would be my permanent family, but I had learned what I needed to learn. I believed we all have an internal wisdom that acts as an inner teacher, and it was time to trust this teacher within. In 1985 I broke up with Roy, crossed the border back into the U.S., and headed into the deserts of New Mexico. I hoped to work with another independent rebirther there and work collaboratively to spread this transformative work.

Chapter 12:
Land of Enchantment

Scared is what you're feeling. Brave is what you're doing.
—Emma Donoghue

The train pulled into the little Amtrak station in Albuquerque. I had watched the landscape change as the train snaked from Washington through Oregon and California and headed east across Arizona and New Mexico. I had never been to New Mexico before, this land of high mesas and infinite sky, this land of Georgia O'Keeffe, who found her artistic life's purpose in the muted colors, the distinct quality of sunlight on the mesas under wide open skies, and her bold visions. She came alive in New Mexico and breathed beauty in all that she saw and painted.

Lucy welcomed me at the station. Getting off the train, I felt the dry desert summer heat on my body. I saw her tall slender figure, short blond hair, and bright smile. She looked like an oasis for this tired body after being on the train for so long. (Was it two days? Longer? It was my first train trip; I had miscalculated my endurance and not reserved a sleeping car.) When we got into her SUV, she handed me a bottle of water. Like I said, an oasis. When we reached her house and went inside, my skin felt refreshed by the swamp cooler, which adds much needed moisture into the air in homes there. At an altitude of 5,300 feet, Albuquerque is high-desert country, so the sun burns with more intensity than at sea level. It took me several days to adjust to the altitude. I tired easily. The dry air sucked moisture from my skin, and I quickly learned the necessity for sunscreen, moisturizer, and carrying water whenever we left the house.

Lucy had been a successful rebirther in the Vancouver community. After completing training, she built a thriving practice. However, a dispute with the leaders compelled her to leave Canada to strike out on her own. I don't remember if there was a personality conflict or an issue of competitiveness or something else. When I arrived in dusty, dry Albuquerque, her life was in full bloom. She had established a rebirthing practice and a network of supporters, including the local new-age bookstore. Also, she was happily married. I was delighted to see her doing so well. Over the next few weeks, I met her friends and others working in the healing arts. People welcomed me with open arms and hearts.

Moving to a new city is transformative. Literally. No one knows your past, whether it's full of failures or successes, mediocrity or excellence. No one knows your insecurities or flaws. You arrive fresh and unblemished. People are willing to see you in a positive light. They will believe the best in you because they want you to reflect the best in them. It's empowering and liberating to believe you can be your best self, that possibility can become reality.

I had experienced this in Vancouver. Now I felt a similar sense of empowerment in Albuquerque, but even stronger. The landscape was completely unfamiliar. Growing up on an island, I had never seen such wide open spaces and so much undeveloped land. I was familiar with bright, vibrant colors in the landscape, lots of trees of all sizes and shapes, the towering firs and pines of British Columbia, endless shades of green, life-giving bodies of water. My eyes needed to recalibrate to appreciate this new pastel environment: sage, coral, pink, lavender, sand, tan, apricot, ochre. They also sought in vain for a lake or river. My disappointment reminded me that I have always lived near water. Lucy was giving me a tour, and as we drove, I asked, "What are those bushes? They're everywhere." She replied, "Those are *trees*. Piñon trees." Oops. Yes, I had arrived in a foreign land.

I knew I was jumping off a cliff in starting a solo rebirthing practice—one without the support of a community, without the guidance of teachers. I was drawn here because I knew Lucy. Adventure was calling; I thought I was ready to live somewhere completely alien to me. Lucy was the only rebirther in town and had built a successful practice. I was eager to follow in her footsteps.

After moving into a house in downtown Albuquerque with one of Lucy's friends, I bought a car and looked forward to my new life in New Mexico. This felt right. This is where I needed to be. Lucy was happy to have a colleague, while I was grateful for her introduction into a new community. I got busy establishing a practice, but it took me a few months to fully appreciate New Mexico and all that offered. I scheduled a few workshops and attracted clients. The art of the Southwest also beckoned me: the iconic pottery, the turquoise and silver jewelry, the numerous art galleries. I also felt pulled to see the pueblos and learn about the local indigenous culture.

In contrast to the alien landscape, I felt a connection to the indigenous peoples living here. Their faces resembled those of my ancestors and my own. Their spiritual relationship to the land reminded me of the Hawaiian people back home and their struggles to maintain their cultures. The numerous native tribes still living in this part of the country were a palpable presence: Zuni, Hopi, Navajo, Santa Clara, Jemez, Acoma, Laguna, Zia, Santo Domingo, Nambé, Cochiti, Apache, and many more. When visiting the ancient ruins of the Anasazi people at Chaco Canyon, I walked through the great houses and sacred kivas of this ancient city. Pottery shards gave evidence of a civilized people, who had designed and built the city to accommodate thousands of inhabitants around 2,000 years ago when it was open land. It's now known as Four Corners where the states of Utah, Colorado, Arizona, and New Mexico meet. I could feel the energy in this place, stronger in some locations than others. It was quiet and not overrun by tourists, so I sat and meditated and felt the sacredness of the land, the forces of life and death in this unforgiving landscape.

New Mexico was the right place for me. However, I began to miss Roy terribly. I wrote and told him I was still in love with him. He had, of course, already moved on and had a new girlfriend. I kept writing. What I didn't reveal, what I could barely admit to myself was that I felt tainted and unclean. I could not imagine dating anyone. Who would want to be with someone with herpes? Even though herpes was fairly common among sexually active adults, I was emotionally paralyzed realizing disclosure was required if I began to care for someone, someone I might be intimate with. I didn't want to infect anyone, that's for sure. In my fear and insecurity, I clung to Roy and the love I thought we had shared.

I thought Lucy and I shared similar goals, that we both wanted to work independently from those in Vancouver and model a different kind of organization, one more egalitarian and less dependent on teachers. Instead, I was disappointed to learn that she wanted to build a community and be in control as a leader/teacher. She wanted to replicate the hierarchical model she had learned in Vancouver. When she told me she had reconnected with the community leaders there, I was speechless. Her desire for more and greater success was familiar. I had witnessed and supported other people and organizations in my past on their roads to riches, with little or no recognition for my contributions. Besides which, this smacked more about business goals than spiritual work. Being successful and being spiritual were not oppositional, however, a fine line existed between the two that could lead to exploiting vulnerable people. Monetizing spiritual work was far too easy; I had left Vancouver and my spiritual community because of doubts regarding the teachers' motivations in this area. Now I questioned Lucy's. I was clear that this was not my path, and upon arriving in Albuquerque, I had formally severed ties with the Empyrean rebirthing community in a letter to its leaders, which I hoped was both honest and loving. Nevertheless, within seven or eight months, my journey into this land of light brought darkness— disillusionment and disenchantment.

I was low on funds and low in spirits. I sank into a depression, utterly lost and unsure about what to do. This was definitely Lucy's turf. Should I stay or leave? I longed for home, for a respite in Honolulu, but didn't have enough money. Not wanting to ask anyone for a loan, I felt completely trapped. I had never felt so desperate, so helpless. Somehow, I had always figured a way out of difficult situations in the past and had never needed to ask my parents for help. I had never *wanted* to ask them for help. To do so would have felt like admitting failure and weakness, which would prove Dad was right about me. What if they said no? I felt so broken already; could I risk feeling worse than I already did? Was it even possible? At the same time, I couldn't go on like this and had to do something, so I wrote them a letter and asked if I could come home for a week or two. I told them I didn't have money for the plane fare and asked for help. I was in agony until I received a reply. Like crawling across broken glass to get to safe ground. They sent me a check for a roundtrip airfare. I dissolved into a puddle of humility, gratitude, and love.

I don't remember exactly what I wrote in my letter. I'm sure I didn't go into detail about my circumstances. Still, they heard my pain, and that was enough for them. And for me. I was both stunned and ecstatic. I really had no idea if they would help me. They did. Me, they were helping me! Glimmers of hope began growing inside me.

Flying over the beautiful Pacific Ocean and seeing the green mountains of Oʻahu and the city of Honolulu below—what a vision for this battered, parched soul! I'd been away far too long. My skin felt rejuvenated by the sweet, moist air. I relaxed in the familiar tropical environment. Subdued during this return to my parents and their home, I was in a vulnerable and uncertain state. It was unavoidable and I had to sit with it. Within days, I knew what to do: leave Albuquerque and return to the Northwest. I also had to ask Dad for a loan to cover the moving expenses and transition time until I could find a job. I still believed in the spiritual principles that I had learned and in the value of rebirthing for personal transformation, but it was clear that I had to work in the actual world instead of sequestering myself in a "special community." I had to see if I could integrate the spiritual teachings I believed in while living in the world like everyone else. After getting settled in Seattle and finding a job, I would start making payments to Dad.

I didn't know that this would be the last time I would see Dad. He did not ask questions about my life or why I didn't have any money. That would have been out of character. However, he did mention that other siblings had borrowed money from him and never repaid him, and he was not happy about their behavior. Point taken; I would not make that mistake.

One day, we were sitting in the living room and Dad expressed his disappointment in my three older brothers. Dad had lavished them with attention, with money. He gave more of himself to them, but I suppose he also expected more. Years after my brothers were well-established in their careers, he brought this up.

Dad was shaking his head. "Your brothers, they could have been lawyers, doctors, businessmen—anything they wanted. But they talked to their teachers about their careers. And what happened? Those teachers encouraged them to be teachers like themselves!

"*Gunfunnit!* My three sons—all teachers! I was so mad. What right did they have? I'm their father, not them. I blame those teachers, they had no right. No right."

He needed to get this off his chest. I listened, surprised at this outburst and having nothing to say. I glanced at his face and his eyes were red. The pain was obviously still fresh.

Every Chinese father wants his sons to be successful in professional fields, but Dad especially wanted one of them to be an engineer, to achieve his own unfulfilled ambition. This was no secret, but my brothers weren't interested. Perhaps they were rebelling against Dad's control. Filial piety went unquestioned when Dad was growing up in Gung Gung's house, but these were different times.

One of my brothers received his doctorate from Stanford and become a college professor. But this was little consolation. The real hurt lay in his sons' dismissal of his fatherly advice. Ironically, his daughters had not become teachers, but had ventured into other professions. My sisters worked in graphic arts and occupational therapy.

My three older brothers had attended St. Louis High School. Dad would not make the same mistake with his fourth son. He enrolled Harry at 'Iolani School, and he must have felt gratified when Harry became an electrical engineer.

In his indirect way of communicating, was Dad letting me know he too had made mistakes? Did he want me to know that it was okay that I had made mistakes, that he knew my life had been challenging? In any case, it was a moment unlike any other when he revealed his heart to me.

Rapprochement? I didn't recognize it then. But, yes, I like to think so. If I had not felt so broken and desperate, I would not have made this visit. I would not have experienced my parents' support and love. I would not have had this moment with my father. I would not have felt a sense of renewal and clarity for my next steps. Turning to my parents as an adult in my late thirties had been gut-wrenching. Unexpectedly, it turned out to be life-affirming.

I returned to the desert to make arrangements to leave. I had lived in Albuquerque less than a year, but it was enough time for the desert to strip away my conceits. To die and be reborn. To trust myself with a heightened consciousness. When I drove away from Albuquerque, I left feeling thankful for the friends I had made there, for the lessons learned. I closed this chapter on rebirthing, ready for a new beginning.

Part 3: Keiki O Ka ʻĀina
(Child of the Land)

Chapter 13:
Land of Volcanoes

There is something infinitely healing in the repeated refrains of nature—the
assurance that dawn comes after night, and spring after winter.
—Rachel Carson

In 1986, not yet 40, I already felt old. I arrived in Seattle after nearly a year
in Albuquerque—high desert country that had humbled me. Hoping
for personal growth and spiritual renewal in the desert, instead I felt
desiccated: Friends and work came and went; the climate and environment
were harsh on my skin, on my soul. Perhaps if I had stayed, my experience
would have evolved into something else, but my thoughts got stuck on "being
lost in the desert." I became ill and depressed before realizing I needed to
leave. After loading up my Mazda sedan, I drove through Arizona and up the
West Coast on I-5, to Seattle, to start all over again—to find somewhere to
live, a job, and a new purpose.

Before arriving in Seattle, which is home for me now, I didn't know
about the volcanoes that punctuate the surrounding mountain ranges: the
Cascades to the east of Seattle and the Olympics to the west. I felt empty and
parched and grateful for the proximity of so much water: Lake Washington,
Lake Union, the Puget Sound, and the Pacific Ocean beyond the Sound. And
so much greenery! Sky-reaching evergreen trees nurtured by the showers
and mists of the ongoing Rain Festival. The Pacific Northwest provided a
welcome contrast to the dry climate and muted colors of the Southwest. And
yet, the gray gloom that can persist into June, also known here as "Junuary,"
and the evergreen mountains were alien to this transplanted islander.

Although not the tropics of my girlhood, I found myself living
once again among volcanoes. Known as Koma Kulshan ("the steep white
mountain") to early Nooksack Indians, Mount Baker rises 10,781 feet north
of Seattle. Closer to the city, Mount Rainier is 54 miles southeast, and Mount

St. Helen's is another 42 miles south of Rainier. While all are cone-shaped stratovolcanoes, Mount St. Helen's cone had collapsed in May 1980 with a violent ash explosion and pyroclastic flow that shaved 1,300 feet off its peak, making its present-day height 8,365.

Mount Rainier is the most visible from Seattle. At 14,411 feet, a sighting of this white glacial mass never fails to make me gasp. Its presence seems other worldly, and I long for this manifestation of something beyond my everyday life—something greater than me or my life, and even greater than humanity. The mountain is always there whether visible or not. What could be more solid than a mountain? Yet, it is often obscured by mist, clouds, rain. When it disappears from the landscape, it leaves a scent of mystery, reminding me of something ethereal, like the mists that often shroud Rainier's peak. It's a beautiful mountain and I have visited it several times over the years—it's very real, very solid. Yet it transcends this world.

Various Pacific Northwest tribes called this Great White Mountain by different names. Some acknowledge it as the source of nourishment and water (Takhoma or "the breast of milk-white water" according to the Yakama people) while others, its proximity to the sky, indicating nearness to the Divine (Ta-ko-bid according to the Puyallup tribe).

On a clear, blue-sky day, the kind that makes you feel reborn, peaceful yet jubilant, I have been over water, perhaps driving across Lake Washington on the I-90 Bridge or traveling on a Washington state ferry, when suddenly Mount Baker, 150 miles away, becomes visible to the north and Mount Rainier to the south.

This is a quintessential Seattle moment: to be in a twentieth-century vessel engineered by human imagination and suspended over water—a vastness carved out by the millennial crawl of glaciers across the landscape; to be between blue above and blue below; to be between two white monoliths of nature, two grand volcanoes. I feel at once diminished and larger than life, with the power to expand my heart to hold all this external beauty inside me.

~~~

Seattle has been good to me over the decades. I have shaped a new life for myself, realized some dreams, and surrounded myself with good friends and strong women who support me through the vagaries of life. This place has provided natural beauty, time, and distance to consider my life in the shadows of mighty volcanoes, to understand what happened to me as a girl and how I managed to survive.

Chapter 14:
Seattle: Making a Circle

We are not trapped or locked up in these bones. No, no. We are
free to change. And love changes us. And if we can love one
another, we can break open the sky.
—Walter Mosley

Beginnings and Endings go together. Like Yin and Yang, they are two sides of the same phenomenon. A door closed for me in Albuquerque. Another opened in Seattle. It was a fresh start. A new beginning.

In the Northwest corner of the United States, on the edge of the Pacific Ocean, Seattle's native name is derived from Chief Seattle of the Duwamish and Suquamish native peoples. Nestled in towering evergreens and skyscrapers dripping with dampness, Seattle cannot hide its indigenous roots. This is beautiful country and no one can deny the splendor of its mountains and lakes, its flora and fauna. Many are drawn to a wide variety of outdoor activities although I suspect they come not solely for recreational purposes. They come to satisfy a profound need for a closeness with Nature, to connect with sacred space. Perhaps even to be reminded that we humans are merely one part of something truly immense, complex and incomprehensible.

Leaving my rebirthing community felt like I had lost a limb. It was painful, but necessary. As I constructed a new life, I grieved. I felt vulnerable. With only a few hundred dollars to my name, I had to adjust quickly—get my bearings and land a job. I stayed for about a week with a former Honolulu rebirther who had moved to Washington. Quickly, I found temp work as an administrative assistant in a company that manufactured lenses for cataract patients and rented a room from a young family. After settling into my new life, I identified another need. Even though I was functional and had the basics in a few weeks—a job, a place to live, and friendly acquaintances, my spirit yearned for support and community. While I was averse to joining any groups or group activities in Seattle for the first year or two, I explored a few options, including talk therapy and a Reiki workshop that gave me the tools to practice this energy work on myself and others. Then I met Terri, a young woman involved in a women's circle.

Terri and I both arranged travel for our bosses as part of our admin roles. In that capacity, Terri and I traveled to Anchorage. We were chatting on the flight back to Seattle when she told me about her group. "We focus on women's empowerment and practice various spiritual beliefs, mostly nature-based ones like those of native peoples and other pre-Christian cultures that worshipped the Great Mother." This intrigued me and, of course, I was familiar with the power in nature embodied in Pele. I also shared the group's interest in Native American spirituality; I had experienced a special energy in the pueblos and ancient kivas in New Mexico and participated in sweat lodges. Reading *The Mists of Avalon* had profoundly affected me a few years earlier in its depiction of patriarchal institutions replacing and exterminating pagan religions based on the Goddess, often with violence.

I took a risk, or perhaps an intuitive leap, by asking if I could join them. It was a small, intimate group meeting in homes. Carol, Janet, Julianne, Karen, Terri and I introduced ourselves briefly. We came from various backgrounds, work experiences; some married, others not; two of us were childless. The six of us sat in a circle in Terri's dimly lit living room. As host, Terri lit five candles invoking the four directions and the center and acknowledged the spirits above and below and the elements connected to the directions. The air smelled of wax and smoke from the burning of dried sage and sweetgrass that we used to smudge our bodies to purify ourselves as we transformed this room into a sacred and safe space, a place where we could let go of our mundane lives and share our secrets and our truths. Little did I know that in this womb-like environment, these women would become my midwives, assisting me in being reborn into my Seattle life.

Finding this women's circle provided much-needed spiritual support, as important to me as food or air or water. We made time to meet every week for a few hours to share our personal stories, support each other through personal crises, and remind each other about the healing wisdom and power of women's' roles in ancient times, claiming these for ourselves. We learned the power of ceremony. We acknowledged Nature's cycles—like our monthly blood and the seasons of the year—to affirm our connection to Nature and to the sacred; everything has cycles, everything changes. This group gave me firm grounding and spiritual support to redefine myself in the real world, in contrast to the insularity in the rebirthing community. I especially appreciated the lack of hierarchy as we shared and rotated leadership roles each week. We acknowledged the sacred in our lives no matter what was going on. Over a few years, some women left and others joined; inevitably further changes occurred that eventually caused the group to disband. However, two of these women have remained in my life.

Gaining more confidence in myself, I auditioned for and joined the Seattle Peace Chorus, fulfilling another goal: to sing. We rehearsed every week, learning songs for public concerts held several times a year. This community choral group traveled to foreign countries as unofficial ambassadors, connecting with ordinary people like ourselves and believing in the common language of music. I didn't read music so I asked another soprano to play the music on the piano so I could record it and practice at home. From our shared dedication to music and this woman's willingness to assist me, a friendship grew. Making music and finding my voice gave me much pleasure and expanded my network. Sometimes our rehearsals went poorly, yet during the performance, our voices, perhaps forty or fifty, blended together and soared as the director had envisioned—it was exhilarating!

Returning to college seemed an impossible dream while working full-time, but it kept invading my thoughts during these early years in Seattle. One day, the heavens parted. The University of Washington established a start-up site in the Bothell business park where I was working. My employer, Interchecks, had a tuition-reimbursement program to encourage employees to continue their education. Suddenly my concerns about having to commute to the Seattle campus and being able to afford the tuition vanished, so I had no more excuses. With a supportive boss, all signs pointed "Go!" I applied, was accepted, transferred my credits from the University of Hawai'i, and started taking one class per quarter. This meant I could not continue with the chorus and its demanding schedule.

I started in an interdisciplinary program in 1991. I had forgotten that when I was 17 and applying to colleges, I leaned toward interdisciplinary programs, so I came full circle in my high-school vision of college. A year or so later, when Interchecks was purchased by a competitor, the office closed and everyone was laid off. It was a difficult transition. However, this meant I could become a full-time student and accelerate the completion of my degree. I applied the severance package I received toward tuition fees.

In the beginning, returning to classes challenged my very core. With just one class per quarter, I quickly learned how rigorous the classes were. I was in my early forties and began doubting my abilities and confidence to continue. Could I manage to read the reams of material and textbook assignments plus re-learn how to write academic papers? I persisted. Perimenopause presented another challenge, throwing my body off-kilter and scrambling my hormones. I suffered through emotional surges, changes in my normal menstrual cycle reminiscent of my early years of menstruation, including cramping, and an acuteness in hearing that disrupted my normal deep sleep: The ambient noises of the apartment building kept me awake. I persisted, even with little sleep. Fortunately, every student was not twenty-something; many working adults, some older than me, were enrolled at this campus—a welcome diversity of ages. Assisted by campus counseling, I was determined to do this.

My identity as an Asian American changed profoundly when I enrolled in a class on Asian American literature and history. Being Chinese did not mean I was aware of the important events and places in Asian American history. For example, I learned about the discriminatory laws that specifically targeted Chinese and Japanese: The Chinese Exclusion Act of 1882 and the National Origins Act of 1924 were enacted to prevent immigration from China and Japan while immigrants from European countries continued to pour into the United States. Another example: When Chinese immigrants were allowed to enter the United States, they were held at a detention center on Angel Island in San Francisco Bay. They could be held there indefinitely, sometimes for years. These pieces of American history apparently were not important to those historians writing textbooks.

However, a Japanese American historian filled this void of Asian Americans in the story of America by writing a book of these invisible Americans, and I was grateful to get my hands on Ron Takaki's *Strangers from a Different Shore* for my class. In primary and secondary school, I had learned little Hawaiian history while the rest of my schooling featured an Anglo or Western civilization perspective, both world and United States, ancient and modern. Minorities were just that—minor and did not matter. No wonder I kept asking myself: *Where do I belong? Where do I fit in?* People who looked like me did not have a place in history books. We were silenced and invisible.

In this class, I found out otherwise: Asian Americans had written novels and poetry to reflect their often-troubled bicultural experiences. Their issues of self-identity were mine. I too was trying to sort out Chinese traditional

112

values centered around the family from American cultural values focused on the individual. I saw myself being a Chinese non-traditionalist in an American context, emphasizing the individual, but here too, it was risky: Women could not be too independent. This was no easy task. What was more important to me: group acceptance or my own self-defined sense of identity?

During the quarter, I realized a strong desire to reconnect with Asian American people. At this point, I had lived in Seattle for about seven years and had several good friends. Still, when I looked around at my friends, classmates, and co-workers, I saw a sea of white faces. Fortunately, Seattle's population is somewhat diverse. It was May, which is designated as Asian Pacific Islander Heritage month, and I attended an event sponsored by the Asian Pacific Islander Women's Network. For the first time since moving to Seattle, I was in a room full of people who looked like me. After the event I joined this women's network.

While I had been working in the private sector in information technology departments, many of these women worked for various social services agencies, such as Seattle Rape Relief and Big Sisters, or in the public sector. They had also immigrated to Seattle from other parts of the country or other countries. Although their backgrounds were different from mine, we shared common ground. This community of women reaffirmed and continue to reaffirm me as a Chinese American woman.

~~~

I step into the cozy elegance of Denise's home—the bamboo wooden floors, the white silk kimono hanging on the wall, and an array of family photos on the fireplace mantle. I've spent many pleasant afternoons here with other Asian Pacific Islander women. Many have joined us over the past few years, but only five of us made a commitment to come together and play mah jongg every month—no excuses! We were determined to learn to play this game with some level of proficiency. Although it's not difficult, it requires practice. Actually, playing MJ was a good reason to pause from our busy lives and be in the company of Asian women. These gatherings were like the brass ring on my merry-go-round life—my monthly reward for surviving a grueling schedule of university classes, sky-high homework, and a full-time office job.

Loud sizzling followed by the pungent aroma of garlic and ginger in hot oil greet me. I breathe deeply and shake off the bone-chilling dampness of a winter Seattle day. Over more sizzling, I hear Denise. "Come in. Come in. I'm in the kitchen."

As I remove my boots, coat, scarf, hat and gloves, Denise emerges from the kitchen. She looks impeccable—silk blouse and slacks, stylish hair and makeup all in place. She was a working mom with multiple responsibilities, and she impressed me in how well she managed the details of her life. More than well. I know she has cleaned the house to welcome her guests and asked her husband to watch their two young children while she has an afternoon with girlfriends. Now she's preparing our lunch.

It's been a month since we last saw each other and we hug with genuine warmth. I follow her into the kitchen. "What can I do?"

"Nothing. Everything's done," she says as she turns off the stove and dishes out the steaming long beans and fresh tofu. In one graceful movement, the dish is on the table. My stomach rumbles softly. I hate arriving somewhere hungry and I hate being late. At least I'm on time. I had eaten breakfast and shouldn't be hungry, but that seems a long time ago.

The rice is cooked and on the table. Hot water is ready for tea. I grab a dish from the cupboard for the green salad with sesame oil dressing I've brought. The rice crackers will be for snacks later.

The others arrive and pull off their cold-weather outer gear. We greet each other—more hugs and big smiles. In addition to Denise and me, Hye-Kyung, Judy, and Anna comprise this dedicated group of players. We move to the dining room, so that those newly arrived can set more food on the table; out of bags and boxes come Korean sushi, pot stickers, and Shanghai green barley noodles. Plates, napkins, and chopsticks are already waiting. We're all hungry and don't need any encouragement to eat. Talking stops abruptly as we fill our plates and our mouths.

The lightly salted seaweed that wraps the rice rolls has been toasted in sesame oil and its fragrance tickles my nose; yellow pickled daikon contrasts with cooked orange carrots, bright-green spinach, and pale yellow scrambled eggs in the center of the sliced sushi. The long beans are cooked perfectly—still slightly crunchy—and the soft tofu is a flavorful mix of ginger, garlic, and salty-sweet hoisin sauce. Pan-fried pot stickers filled with pork and vegetarian ones for Hye-Kyung are next to a dish with piquant Chinese black vinegar for dipping. The freshly-made shaved noodles are oval-shaped, soft yet firm. Young barley shoots give them a pleasant light green shade. Cooked greens, carrots, onion, and scrambled eggs are mixed in a delicate sauce of soy and garlic with the noodles. On the plate, all the sauces meld together, and it's not possible to keep each course separate. Good food is essential for our get-togethers.

Half an hour goes by as we eat and chat. Denise asks, "Have you heard about the new Korean restaurant that just opened on Aurora Avenue?"

"Oh yeah, you know my sister—she's always up with the latest restaurants." Hye-Kyung reports, "She says it's already popular with the Korean church crowd. They love the home-style comfort food."

"Sounds good. We should go!"

The afternoon had barely begun, and we're already looking forward to our next meal together.

After lunch fills our bellies, we gather around the card table and dump the mah jongg tiles out of the case. The sound of them clicking against each other conjures up the good times we've had with each other. It's time to begin playing, time to wash the tiles.

The tiles lie in a jumble in the middle of a card table. The four players reach in to begin washing the tiles, moving their hands in a circular direction and pushing the tiles toward the center. It's like shuffling a pack of playing cards except this is a group activity in mah jongg, not an individual one. Washing the tiles starts a new game. It's a new beginning.

Having strong women in my life, especially strong Asian women, has propelled my own development as a woman. Community activism, the pursuit of higher education and the arts, women's rights and health—these were important themes in all our lives.

~~~

Other university classes impressed me, shaping and expanding my awareness. I visited Washington, D.C. for the first time during a human rights class where we met with diplomats, congressional representatives, and leaders of non-governmental organizations to hear different perspectives about human rights issues and abuses. The feminist thought and theory class opened my eyes to women's history and issues and made me realize my own battles with gender bias in my family were only one example in a broader context of the oppression of women. And for three quarters I had a work-study job at the writing center where undergrad and graduate students came to tackle the challenges of writing a thesis and other academic papers. When I first started, I had certainly struggled with this myself, and now I could help others.

After completing my bachelor's degree, I decided it was time to write the stories I've been wanting to write. As an administrative and executive assistant at various companies over the past nine years, I had produced a slew of business documents. Now I started to write personal stories and vignettes about growing up in Honolulu. I joined writing groups and met other writers, including Holly, who had been a resident at a writing retreat for women writers in the woods of Whidbey Island, a bit north of Seattle. She was ecstatic about her experience there; she felt nurtured and supported as a woman writer, and she urged us emerging writers of color in the group to apply to Hedgebrook for a residency.

A few years later, I did and was accepted. It was an intimate group of six women; we each had a cozy, private cottage nestled in the woods and heated by a wood-burning stove. The act of building a fire was both practical and extraordinary. As I sat at the long built-in desk in this perfectly efficient, hand-crafted cottage, I was hoping a creative spark would ignite into words flowing onto the page, to emerge as the writer that Hedgebrook believed me to be. I was working on the first manuscript of this memoir. We six writers of various genres, prose and poetry, convened for dinner in the farmhouse each evening and shared our writing, our stories. One woman came from Zimbabwe. Her quiet presence gave me a window into the larger world of women writers. Connecting to another writer who lived on a far-away continent and who was committed to her art despite extreme economic and political turmoil in her daily life—this was inspiring beyond words.

Hedgebrook gave me another community of women—thankfully in Seattle and the surrounding region, but also nationally and internationally. This was an unexpected bonus. The generous gift of the residency—time and solitude to write in a safe and nurturing environment, as well as validation as a writer—was remarkable and life-changing.

Choosing Seattle as a new home was mostly a gut feeling. I had no awareness what fertile literary soil I was planting myself into. People here love their books and bookstores. Book clubs are epidemic. Independent bookstores include neighborhood stores as well as larger venues like The Elliott Bay Book Company and Third Place Books, where author readings fill monthly calendars. I attended a few readings most weeks, as part of my "post-graduate studies." I soon learned that writers, who could engage readers on the page, did not necessarily perform well in person. I learned a writer needs many skills. I also saw that writers come in all shapes, sizes, and colors. Maybe, just maybe, I could be one too.

Many writing communities proliferate here. Perhaps the gloom that descends on the area for much of the year contributes to solitary and reflective pursuits. Seattle has a literary arts center (Hugo House) and one of only two poetry bookstores (Open Books) in the country. Writers can enroll in numerous writing workshops and conferences anytime of the year. In addition, I've learned that the city, county, state, and various non-profit arts organizations encourage artistic endeavors by offering grants. Writers can receive funding to generate new work, offer workshops, and attend residencies.

In 1986 when I first arrived, I had no awareness of the looming computer revolution or Seattle's role in this technology boom; this area would be labeled the Silicon Forest when Microsoft became a household word. At my first job, I landed in the information systems department of a lens manufacturing company and was introduced to the personal computer: a dark screen with a flashing cursor. Those were primitive days. This initiation into computer skills and being around techies gave me an advantage in subsequent jobs.

~~~

In addition to my cultural roots as a Chinese American woman, I reconnected to my Hawaiian roots. While I am not ethnically Hawaiian, Hawai'i lives in my body and heart. I met Joan Na'ilima, whose Hawaiian lineage comes through her mother's family. She lives near the Canadian border of Washington, but she was born and raised on Moloka'i and attended Kamehameha Schools in Honolulu. Two island women, we became friends; she raised my awareness about the many people from Hawai'i, who have resettled in Washington and other parts of the Northwest. Various Hawai'i clubs, hula hālau, and outrigger canoe clubs provide numerous activities and events to keep these transplanted islanders connected to the islands and Hawaiian culture.

Before my commencement ceremony in June 1995, Joan and I went to Golden Gardens Park near Seattle for a Hawaiian cultural event. Here I was to receive an unexpected gift. However, it would be more than a decade before I fully appreciated its significance.

~~~

Graduating from the university was a huge milestone. A culmination of hard work, hopes, and dreams—decades-long dreams. And no ordinary completion, but one shiny with multi-colored confetti and brass bands. A gift to myself, enriching my heart and expanding my sense of self, perhaps beyond my physical body, if there really are such things as auras. If so, my aura would have been a field of golden light emanating several feet around me.

Class of 1994! It was a game-changer, beyond what I had hoped for as a teenager. I'd like to say my life was golden from this point onward, but it wasn't so. Life doesn't work that way. It's not a linear timeline, but wavy, with both ups and downs, peaks and valleys. "Happily ever after" is a concept to lift us out of our mundane lives. It's a device for story-telling, and not reality or a model for life and should not be confused with such. Even for those of us who love fairy tales.

Nonetheless, this completion set me on a new path—one that allowed me insight into important themes in my life in the years to come, directing me in making connections with disparate parts of my life, and giving me courage to examine and rethink my personal history. It gave me freedom to be more myself, to take myself seriously, including acknowledging something I've always wanted to do ever since meeting the inimitable Jo March: to pursue creative writing.

During my last year of college I started writing poetry. The poetry was mostly bad, while the writing itself felt validating—to express myself in a form that broke free from academic papers. This early writing released the genie in the bottle; my hidden creativity would not be contained again. I eventually turned to prose, which felt more natural to me. But once in a while, poetry will flow from me unbidden, begging for life on the page.

This act of writing opened up other secret doors inside me. Writing is an act of inquiry. It requires curiosity and an inclination to pursue answers. I had no conscious desire to write a book. My quest was to understand my life and why things had happened the way they happened. Because the writing process is unpredictable, it brought unexpected events, people, and insight into my life.

~~~

The true value of a college education involves more than preparation for a career. My degree did advance my possibilities into jobs such as executive administration/management positions with more responsibilities and higher salaries. However, I value this education primarily because I learned about myself and the world. I gained critical-thinking skills to apply to understanding and navigating through the complexities of life. Also, I acquired an expanded sense of myself and a life wherein I had the confidence to actualize my dreams.

Gaining this insight brought compassion, which fostered a deeper appreciation for my mother. I had discounted her life as a traditional wife and mother; I had rejected her as a role model when I was struggling to figure out my life. Her dependency and restricted lifestyle represented limitations defined and imposed by others. In contrast, I aligned with women who wanted more freedom, more opportunities to live full and complete lives.

I learned, however, that life is rarely so simple, so black and white. Mom had once dreamed about being a doctor. In high school, she developed a hearing problem that prevented her from completing high school. Instead, she went to business school, then found a job at Dad's store. She didn't have the option to choose an independent life, to date someone not Chinese, to marry for love. Women of her generation did not think about family planning or how to prevent becoming pregnant.

Mom did not exhibit any hearing problems until she was in her sixties. It was surprising when she revealed her story. Perhaps it had been a temporary condition or one that was misdiagnosed. Nevertheless, it affected her high school education and demolished her hopes for higher education and a medical career. Yet, she did not dwell on any lost dreams after she became a wife and mother. If she did, it was not obvious to me. Her life was mostly comfortable even though it held challenges she could not articulate, perhaps dared not speak about. And so, I like to think that completing my B.A. represented a victory of sorts, not only for me, but also for those women like my mother who were unable for whatever reason to attend or complete college.

Chapter 15:
About Rape

*Forgive but do not forget, or you will be hurt again. Forgiving
changes perspectives. Forgetting loses the lesson.*
—Paulo Coelho

The Rape, Abuse, and Incest National Network (RAINN) website defines rape as follows:

*Rape is forced sexual intercourse, including vaginal, anal, or oral penetration. Penetration
may be by a body part or an object.*

Rape.

When did I first hear this word?

It might have been when I bought the soundtrack album for the Broadway musical *The Fantasticks*. I was 14 or 15 and loved the songs "Try to Remember" and "Soon It's Gonna Rain." (This song could have been written for Seattle, however, I had no inkling of this place where I would one day live.) The melodies stuck in my head and I hummed them. When my sister Marleen bought the sheet music for these songs, I sat down next to her on the piano bench as she played. I helped her by turning the pages and ventured to sing along.

"Soon It's Gonna Rain" is a sweet love song expressing the desire of two young lovers to find a special place to be together, safely away from their fathers who seemingly oppose their love.

I discovered I liked singing, had a decent voice, and my sister did not shoo me away. Anxious to hear all the music from this popular show, I ordered the album from my record club. When it came in the mail, I rushed to the courtyard to play it on our high-fidelity record player and settled down to enjoy the music, fully confident I would love every song, even the unfamiliar ones. When I heard "The Rape Song," I couldn't believe it. *Was I hearing the words correctly? They're singing about rape? In a light-hearted manner? What...?*

My reaction tells me I had some understanding of the word or I wouldn't have been shocked. No one uttered the word in public, much less *sang* about it. It was like a swear word, not to be spoken in polite company. Yet, this song is performed by the two fathers in the musical play. They are tossing around ideas for bringing their son and daughter together and discussing possible scenarios such as "the rape emphatic" or "the rape polite."

After listening to the entire soundtrack, I understood the story of this long-running Broadway show. It's a convoluted plot. The two fathers actually want the two young people to fall in love, but they think that throwing obstacles in their way will push them together, so in "The Rape Song," they are plotting a fake abduction, not sexual violation, of the daughter.

(Note: This song is no longer performed and has been replaced.)

The word more likely entered my consciousness through reading, perhaps when I discovered several old magazines and books in Gung Gung Lee's house, where Dad grew up. Sitting old and worn-out across our front lawn, this was the house that Gung Gung built in readiness to bring his family, his wife and only son, from China to Honolulu in 1912. He was very proud of this house and property on Pua Lane, a house that years of hard work had paid for.

In my childhood, Gung Gung's house appeared like many fifty-year-olds: faded and sagging in places, generally weathered. After Gung Gung died and some of my father's sisters married and moved out, a new family house was built in 1940. Gung Gung's big house of two stories was partitioned into two rental units. The old sitting room that faced the new house became a storage room for miscellaneous items and keepsakes. Here we found old, dusty issues of magazines and comics, stacks of old books, some rattan furniture, even old trunks from China. It was our version of an attic, which most Honolulu houses lack. We liked rummaging around in this musty storage room. Like a treasure hunt, we didn't know what we might find. *Life* and *Look* magazines depicted events during the war years. And I found a book revealing the Rape of Nanking, the capital city of China during the Second Sino-Japanese War. *Japanese Terror in China* reprinted documents by Western eyewitnesses to the atrocities of 1937 when the Japanese army invaded and captured Nanking. It was compiled by the China correspondent for *The Manchester Guardian* and published in 1938.

Tensions between China and Japan had been smoldering since the end of the nineteenth century, and Japan lay in wait for any excuse to viciously attack China. In 1931 Japan invaded Manchuria and occupied this large region of China, establishing a base to launch further attacks on China in the coming years.

I didn't understand how a city could be raped. I had heard about the concentration camps and the atrocities perpetrated by Nazis in Europe, but these events in Nanking seemed even more disturbing. The rape involved a systematic and prolonged terrorization, brutalization, and depraved violence against an entire city filled with non-combatants: women, girls, the elderly, children, babies—no one was spared. Being shot quickly was a mercy in comparison, even when shot in the back. Not only did all this happen to people of my heritage, but the perpetrators were Asian: Japanese soldiers took license with impunity to behave with unprovoked violence and savagery. Soldiers had killing contests for their amusement, decapitated defenseless civilians. They buried living people up to their heads or chests, trampled over them with horses or tanks, used their swords to hack away at their bodies, or ordered German shepherds to attack them. Their blood lust drove them to murder and torture the Chinese with unnecessary cruelty: running swords through babies and raping children, grandmothers, pregnant women, even those near labor. This was a history unknown to me as a pre-teen, although reports of these events had reverberated in Chinese communities everywhere at the time, including Honolulu, and raised tensions between Chinese and Japanese communities. This was shocking and horrifying.

The citizens of Nanking were murdered and raped. Buildings and homes were looted, bombed, burned. In 1937, Nanking had a population of 1.2 million people. Half of the population fled the city in advance of the Japanese. Of the approximately six hundred thousand people remaining, nearly half died within a six-week period—murdered and often tortured. The other half survived as refugees in a safety zone created by Westerners who chose to remain in order to help the Chinese. The fifteen members of the International Committee for Nanking Safety Zone included Americans, British, Danish, and German citizens. The Japanese military purposefully destroyed everything: people, families, the city, and the culture. They intended to set an example for the rest of China to forestall any resistance to their invasion and occupation.

Despite the weight of documentation, the Japanese Government has never acknowledged these atrocities. Japanese history books are silent about these events.

~~~

The Japanese people I knew in Honolulu were gentle, kind, and hard-working. Japanese families lived in some of our rental houses: the Yamadas, Imamuras, Matsumotos. Many of my classmates were Japanese, including my best friend who rode the bus home with me every day after school to attend a Japanese language school near my house.

Our family bought vegetables, comic books, and shave ice from the neighborhood mom 'n pop grocery stores owned by Japanese families. And, of course, the Japanese delis or okazuyas offered some of my favorite food: maki sushi, sweet potato tempura, nishime, gobo, namasu, and mochi.

I have cousins on both sides of the family who are both Japanese and Chinese. One of the Lee aunties married a young, local Japanese man. One of my mother's brothers married a local Japanese woman. She was actually Okinawan, but I didn't know the difference. It didn't matter. They were all family.

However, my family tree is even more complicated. Mom grew up with two brothers in her adopted family. Grandfather Wong and Grandmother Wong had adopted their three children, including two boys who were biological brothers. I simply assumed these uncles were Chinese like my mother and grandparents. In 1998 my cousin informed me these uncles, one of them his father, were mixed Chinese-Japanese, which was news to my cousin, too. I think my grandparents must have been remarkable people with huge hearts to take in these brothers, whose Japanese blood was problematic for many families in those days.

Then there was Mama-san. When I recall this woman from my childhood, I'm not sure I trust my memory. A small Japanese woman, she came to our house perhaps three times a week to help my mother with domestic chores like the laundry and housecleaning, sometimes babysitting.

I remember her as an older woman with graying hair although she probably wasn't that old when I first knew her as a pre-school child. She wore a light hair net to keep her hair neat while working. She had a distinctive smell: clean like freshly ironed clothes. Her dresses were sensible: simple shirtwaists, V-neck, no collar, cotton, with a small all-over print in subdued or neutral colors. She probably sewed her own and her family's clothes. She put on a white muslin apron over her dress when she arrived.

Because we called her "Mama-san" and she was a regular presence in our home, I thought she was a relative. Children have little awareness about a person's social status, so I had no idea that she came to our house as a paid domestic worker. When we saw her walking down the driveway approaching the house, my sister and I would run to greet her yelling, "Mama-san! Mama-san!" with a genuine affection that she returned unconditionally.

Her voice had a Japanese accent when she spoke Pidgin English; she always spoke in a calm manner. If we were fighting with each other, she might pull one of us away and say, "No hit, no hit. She your sistah." She cooled our anger by giving us a little chore to distract us from the argument. "Come, come. Help me." We weren't really helping her; she didn't require our help. Still, it felt like we were being useful and our anger soon faded.

If we weren't playing, we liked hanging around her, probably getting in her way, but she never made us feel we were nuisances. She had a little table and chair in the laundry room near the door to the back yard where the clotheslines stood silently at attention. Here in the laundry room is where she left her purse, her bento lunch, and personal things when she came at the beginning of the day and where she hung up her apron at day's end. Here is where she ate her lunch. She unwrapped the cloth she used to carry the small, stacked aluminum bento boxes and took out her chopsticks. "Come, come. You like try?" Her chopsticks would offer us a piece of pickled radish or she might give us a musubi with a salty plum in the middle. The riceball wrapped in seaweed was simple food. Eating Mama-san's food was always a treat.

~~~

These were the Japanese people I knew: they were our neighbors, our friends and classmates, our relatives, the families who owned neighborhood businesses, and the woman who came into our home to help my mother. They enriched my everyday life, so I had difficulty believing that other Japanese people far away during the war had exhibited such reprehensible behavior, murderous and savagely violent. Thankfully, war is incomprehensible to most children. Of course, the local Japanese population was not responsible for the behavior of the Japanese Imperial Army in China. They had no connection to the terrorism and rapes used as weapons of war to massacre and demoralize the Chinese. However, the anger and outrage of the expatriate Chinese community, who felt entirely helpless, needed an outlet and blame found convenient targets.

In my father's family, Gung Gung Lee disowned a daughter for dating a young, local Japanese man during these tense times. He would not tolerate either a child's disobedience or such blatant disregard for the suffering of the Chinese in the old country at the hands of the Japanese army. As a respected personage in Chinatown, he would not lose face in his community because of a reckless, ungrateful daughter. He threw her out of the house and she was not allowed home again.

When I was growing up in the Sixties, Dad was a respected businessman in Chinatown. As in any community, people love to gossip. In Gung Gung's day, the 1920s and 1930s, Honolulu was even smaller and news traveled quickly via the "coconut wireless." Gung Gung had his reputation to uphold, not only locally, but also in the broader Chinese community—as far away as San Francisco, Hong Kong, and wherever he had business contacts.

This period of the Second Sino-Japanese War was a painful time for my family and Chinese people everywhere. I have no doubt that what happened to Dad's sister strongly influenced my father when I defied him by dating a young white man. Dad was upset, but he was not going to take the extreme action that Gung Gung had.

I glanced through *Japanese Terror in China* and superficially understood the general events of the Rape of Nanking; I put it aside. I recognized this was an important historic document, but I decided to postpone reading it until I was no longer a child. I know now I wasn't ready to deal with the hellish reality, to read the details of such savagery and depravity witnessed by the survivors. To know of such crimes and such men. Thankfully, the book did not have photos.

~~~

Rape.

When did I first understand I had been raped?

If I even mentioned it, I used other words: "I was molested" or "I was sexually abused." And *that* was difficult enough. I thought being raped meant his penis had to have touched me. And thank goodness I never saw or felt his penis. I was naïve and misinformed. I didn't know that any body part or object used in a sexual act without consent is rape.

The Rape of Nanking was well-documented. The few Westerners who refused to abandon the Chinese risked their own safety. They witnessed the bodies of young and old violated indiscriminately by the enemy with their weapons and whatever objects were available.

When I first started to write about being raped, I considered writing fiction and attended a fiction workshop. The insightful instructor knew I was revealing something deeply personal about myself. He did not mince words when he referred to the events as rape.

 I was stunned. At fifty-nine, I had never used this word in the context of my life. None of my therapists had either. This teacher gently guided me to recognize what happened to me was rape. If I was going to write about something, I had to know what it was. I had to name it. I had to call it exactly what it was.

Rape is such a harsh, ugly word. This is the spelling of how the word feels in my body: rAAApe. The A's form sharp daggers that scratch the flesh in my throat when I say it. I feel the sound cutting me all the way down into my belly. Sometimes it's a gasp, the reflexive need for more air as the word seems to suck the breath out of me. Maybe it's such an ugly word because rape has become too common these days—these acts of violence and power over another, often someone physically smaller, happen every day, everywhere, in both times of peace and in war. Flip the television to a crime show, and odds are good that a woman has been raped.

Rape is not an act of sexual desire. Rape is not the old definition of ritualized bride kidnapping or abduction sung in irony in *The Fantasticks*. Rape is an act of one human dehumanizing another. Rape is the thoughtless killing of another's soul and often the body. Rape is the theft of light from their eyes, replacing it with fear, doubt, and pain.

Rape is forced sexual intercourse, including vaginal, anal, or oral penetration. Penetration may be by a body part or an object.

Understand this: I was only a child. When the perpetrator is an adult and the victim is a child, the child is NOT capable of giving consent to sexual acts. NOT NOT NOT. I did NOT consent. I did NOT even understand what he was doing.

Chapter 16:
Revising Home

We decided that it was no good asking what is the meaning of life,
because life is a question, and you, yourself are the answer.
—Ursula Le Guin

It was time to move again. In March 2010, I gave notice to my landlord, following my instincts even though I had nowhere to go. My studio apartment was small, clean, quiet, and close to friends. Rent was $375 including utilities—a great deal since I wasn't working thanks to the Bush Recession. Having lived here for more than two years, I began to feel confined. I wanted more space to stretch and grow—physically, mentally, and creatively. When I learned my landlord had entered my apartment when I was out of town and failed to inform me before or after, which is the law, I knew it was time to move. Moving is always stressful—a mixture of fear, anxiety, uncertainty, and even loss. Amidst this swirl of feelings, I was compelled to reflect on this idea of home and what home means.

Home is a place, an idea, a set of values. It can be geography, a physical space, or an abstraction.

At its best, home evokes more than mere shelter, more than an address. It's a place of safety, somewhere that is loving and nurturing, a place of sanctuary and healing. Home is not only for the body and its comfort. It's where the soul comes to rest, where peace can be assured and assumed.

Home is all of the above. It's something that lives inside the heart, body, soul. A person may leave a landscape or a place, but can never leave Home.

~~~

Fear shadowed my search. What if I didn't find anything I liked or could afford? At first, I was optimistic as I scanned Craigslist ads online. Rental prices in a bad economy would be down, right? Not necessarily. After a few weeks of looking and rejecting what I saw, I got worried and cranky. My stomach was upset and sleep did not bring rest. I began packing my things with no idea where I was going.

And what was this frequent moving from place to place all about? Every two to four years, I was on the move. I was a decent person and highly responsible, but I seemed to have a nomadic streak. I've rented for most of my life and I suppose renting connotes a temporary situation. Was I needing to define home for myself over and over again? Or was I reconciling a feeling of homelessness resulting from my history of sexual trauma? Did others experience this feeling of homelessness when safety in the home was breached, when innocence was shattered and a feeling of vulnerability became all too real?

Being raped in my childhood home—did this create a divide inside me between home and safety? Is this why it's been so difficult to stay in one place for very long? I wondered how many homeless people have a history of rape and other abuse.

~~~

My family lived in the same house throughout my childhood. We never had to move. After we children grew up and left, my parents continued living there. Mom lived there all of her married life and moved into a condo only a few years after Dad died. The house was too big for one person, especially one in her seventies. She was ready for a change.

My family had all the comforts of a middle-class life. The house was a single-story house of wood raised slightly above ground, high enough so that we had a few steps at both back and front doors. The above-ground-level design pre-empted flooding during tropical storms, ground heat, and creepy-crawly critters like centipedes. Its three bedrooms, kitchen, dining room, living room, and den seemed plenty big to me as a child.

Gung Gung Lee's old house faced Pua Lane, which intersected Vineyard. He bought this property after working many long years separated from his wife and son in China. Because of Gung Gung's vision for a new and better life, our home on Vineyard Street was located in this 1940s house, on this property, in this neighborhood not far from Chinatown, on this beautiful island in the blue Pacific.

~~~

What is this idea of Home? Is it a place? A feeling? Or a state of being? Being at home.

I live in Seattle. Seattle is home, but I was born and raised in Honolulu. No matter where I live, Hawai'i will always be Home. When I say Home I hear Hawaiian music in the background. This is music that opens my heart. It's a place where I know I belong, where I feel whole, where my body and soul are fused. It's a place of warmth and beauty, where I experience safety and well-being, where I can be myself and feel complete.

If Hawai'i is Home and I don't live there, is it enough to know I have a place I can call Home? In this crazy world, I think it is: It's enough to know I belong somewhere. It's enough to feel rooted even though I'm not physically there. I suppose it's like the idea of heaven—for those who believe in heaven—as a place of eternal peace. Hawai'i is not heaven. It's not paradise. It's not an ideal or perfect world. Really. No perfect childhoods, people, or situations exist there. But it embodies an energy that I feel and connect with. I don't know if it's because I was born there and my body is sensitized to the island energy or mana. I intuitively know I have to visit regularly to restore myself in the island's beauty, the ocean, the land.

Hawai'i is a sacred place, a place of healing. I honor its sacredness and it honors me as keiki o ka 'āina. This feeling of reciprocity and respect is powerful. As a child of the land, I am forever linked to this volcanic landscape. I have played in the dirt, in the soil, I have breathed it in, I have eaten the fruits and vegetables grown here. The land is in my body, in my cells. I wonder if Gung Gung Lee felt this connection when he decided to bring over his wife and son instead of returning to settle in China.

~~~

Home is this body. While home has many layers of meaning, ultimately we live in our bodies. Our very first homes were our mothers' bodies, before we entered the world as separate beings. Watching infants and children learn about their fingers and toes reminds me how wondrous our bodies are. Watching a child learn to crawl, then stand up, then take a few steps— it's as monumental as a human walking on the moon. Learning mobility requires lots of mistakes, lots of falling down. A child has such resilience and determination. Nothing will stop her from walking. You can see it in her eyes: I can do it. I can do it.

We all did this. It's a good reminder because during the course of a lifetime, we will land on our butts from time to time. Hopefully we will have others around us who will help us get back on our feet. Who will listen if we need to rant and rave, to curse our gods, to unburden our hearts. Who will offer comfort by their presence and encouraging words to help us take the next step. When I was raped, I intuitively knew what happened was wrong, but my training told me: *Don't bother the adults. Don't tell stories about adults.* I had nowhere to go, no one to tell. I had to keep this locked up inside me where it fell into an abyss and got lost.

As an adult, I recognized this quiet crime. The full gravity and a child's unexpressed grief took longer to surface. And the rage. Not only about the rape, but also my father's behavior; he handed me over to a rapist, a pedophile. Obviously, he did not know this. Still, what could Dad have been thinking? I want to think that he was oblivious about such crimes, especially in his own home. I don't know. I want to think that life was more innocent then, that it would have been inconceivable for an adult to imagine such a scenario. Is such naïveté accurate? Today, no male should be casually left alone with any child. Back then, these crimes were certainly happening whether or not my parents were aware of them. Could Dad have been a victim of sexual abuse himself? I know nothing about his childhood or the people he lived with. What did he really know about his masseur? And why allow him to be alone in a room with me? It would have been easy to ask one of my siblings to stay. I have a vague memory that my older brothers also received sample treatments. Is this accurate? If so, what happened? After his massage, Dad would go to his bedroom to rest and change. While Mr. Kishi was waiting, Dad might have thought it a good idea to keep his masseur busy. Does this make any sense? Why would I think this? Is there a part of me that still wants to think Dad was blameless? He was the parent who should have protected me from harm. *This I do know.*

Dad did not provide a welcoming space for communication, certainly not for me to seek help when something happened that disturbed me. I didn't learn good communication skills in this setting. What I learned was that family was not safe for me. I didn't know how I would learn to be safe in the world, but this home and this family were not good options.

~~~

When I look at old photos of myself as a young woman, I see them with different eyes. I am surprised: I was a lovely young woman. I had so little self-esteem that I only saw what I thought needed improvement. I kept comparing myself to others who were prettier, thinner, taller, fairer, more graceful, more athletic, and on and on.

In my family, I was one of the brownies; I tanned while others retained their fairness. Their teasing taught me that being brown was undesirable. I was an oddity and learned to be at odds with my body. I certainly did not understand my body as I matured into womanhood. Rebelling against my parents as a teenager signified taking control of my life and my body. My sexuality liberated me. The passion in my body compelled me to act like someone different, not my normal passive self. I didn't want to be passive any longer; I wanted to be someone who dared to live fully, unafraid to grab on and ride the roller coaster of life, with screaming permitted. And so, I claimed my body even as I was still learning how to live in it. The learning would continue; more lessons of the body were to come.

~~~

Home can mean family. If you're lucky, you feel at home with your family of origin, your parents and siblings. As an adult, perhaps you marry, have your own children, create a home. Creating home requires intention. It doesn't happen automatically when people come together. When it does happen, home is an act of love and emotional security: Home means people who love and support one another no matter what—mistakes, missteps, poor judgments, and all. Intuitively I know this is possible. My observations and experiences of friends and their families support this. No one has it all figured out, but communication can be learned if people truly care.

What about my family? My siblings and I all left home—for school, for work, for love, for adventure. Five scattered to the East and West coasts of the continental United States. Joleen married and moved to the Big Island. Clyde married and settled in Honolulu. Not coincidentally, geography separated us across the map so that as adults, we rarely gathered at the same time in the same place—islands unto ourselves.

When my parents died, the cracks in the family became fissures, actually crevasses that could swallow a whole person. My siblings morphed into strangers whose behavior was foreign, as if we didn't speak the same language, and sometimes mean-spirited, as if we were children trying to take each other's lunch money. Without my parents, there was no glue to keep us together. I don't like to think our disintegration was inevitable. However, no one had the desire or skills to keep us together, especially with the events following my parents' deaths.

Dad died in 1987. He was 85. After his death, he provided for my mother, who was only 68. However, instead of leaving his estate to his wife of 45 years, he provided her with cash and investments and a residence for as long as she lived. In death he ensured material comfort for Mom, as he had in life.

The remaining assets were placed in a trust: real estate, investments, household items, etc. His will directed how these were to be distributed to his seven children. Dad wanted to leave us an inheritance—a material legacy to prove he was a good father. I presumed that Mom would live many, many more years, and the trust would be depleted to provide for her needs.

Mom had never lived alone. As a widow, she experienced a new freedom. In the beginning, my siblings and I worried about how she would adjust after a lifetime in a house with a husband and children and then only a husband. In truth, she had catered to our needs, and now she was liberated from taking care of others. She was more than fine. She was happy. This is the simple truth. She fulfilled some dreams: traveling to China with my Wong aunties and traveling to various parts of the U.S. with Joleen's family. She could do whatever she wanted whenever she wanted: go shopping, eat her favorite foods, read, watch television. She loved *Law & Order*. She was accountable to no one. Finally.

~~~

Mom had had a hearing problem for decades, but we did not become aware of it until she was in her sixties. Dissatisfied with hearing aids, she gave them up, along with much socializing, except when one of her children came to visit. She loved these visits and loved taking us out to eat. When she moved into a condo, she could easily walk to Chinatown or downtown or take a bus to Ala Moana Shopping Center. In Chinatown, she knew where to buy the best papayas, which she and I enjoyed. One year when I visited, she got us tickets to see the Shanghai acrobats. Despite her hearing loss, she enjoyed life even though most of her children lived on the mainland and phone calls were nearly impossible. Perhaps this is why our visits were so important to her. Except for her interactions with Clyde, her last years living in her condo were quiet and comfortable. She seemed to welcome the solitude of living solo.

In death, Dad continued to divide us by favoring my brothers; only they were to inherit the family property in Honolulu, which was the most valuable asset. After recovering from the shock of the will, my sisters and I requested that we share my father's inheritance in equal shares—all of it. My brothers agreed, but the legal document we requested to ensure this would happen never came to pass. My father had designated one of his sons as the executor of his will, and my brother seemed intent to carry out my father's unfair wishes.

At this time, my mother had no will. One brother suggested she employ his lawyer, but I spoke frankly with her and expressed my concern that he may not have her best interests at heart.

Mom died unexpectedly in 1998. Thankfully, Mom had retained her own lawyer and gotten her legal affairs in order. The most remarkable part of her bequest was this: To guarantee that her daughters were treated fairly by my brother, in his capacity as executor for Dad's estate, Mom stipulated in her will that her beneficiaries would be exclusively her daughters *unless* my brothers shared my father's estate equally among all of us. She took a stand against her husband and her sons for the sake of equity. She had risen up with the power of a tsunami that crashes down on unsuspecting communities. I felt such pride in her courage to defy tradition. But it was messy.

We all agreed to sell the family home and property in Honolulu. Most of us had our own lives away from the islands. Also, no one could afford to buy out the shares of the other siblings. The family home is now gone for good.

~~~

Solidarity with my sisters failed to materialize after Mom's death. One sister and her husband lived in New York. She was upset for a number of reasons, only some of which I knew about. I reached out. We lived on opposite coasts, but I offered to help where I could—a tenuous connection at best.

I thought that if the value of Mom's estate (divided by three) was roughly equal to what we might receive from both estates (divided by seven), we could save ourselves a lot of time and grief by not having to deal with our brother. However, our sister did not respond to a request for financial information regarding Mom's estate. Legally, she didn't have to consult us or invite any discussion. She decided to work toward equal distribution of *both* estates to all siblings. Although she might have felt this was the best course to keep the family intact, this didn't happen. Whether she consulted with her lawyer on this matter, I do not know. What I do know is that she stepped into the fire.

In my opinion, she made an unnecessary sacrifice in exposing herself to years of our brother's abusive behavior, verbal and psychological, in dealing with estate issues. Like the war-wounded, she never discussed the details with me. When she asked for help, I did what I could. She was a daughter and he, a son. In China in another time, he could have crushed her, a lowly female, as easily as killing a mosquito for not submitting to his authority.

Recognizing a pattern of emotional abuse in my family has been eye-opening. This, plus my history of sexual abuse, intensified my vulnerability during these years of conflict more than I realized. Understanding that family discord due to wills, bequests and inheritance matters are fairly common did not lessen the pain that was unnecessarily inflicted.

Ten years after Mom's death, the family was undone for me when both estates were finally settled. Or maybe it was never "done" to begin with. It's a sadness I cannot put into words, but that I have had to learn to live with.

Still, Mom's advocacy for her daughters represented a major victory for Mom and for us, her daughters. This legal document forced my brothers to recognize their sisters as full and equal members of the family. Although coerced, gender equity prevailed after so many years of gender bias, of being disadvantaged and disrespected. I didn't assume that my brothers would suddenly esteem us from this point forward. However, unspoken was the fact that we Lee women would no longer be bullied by the Lee men nor controlled by male privilege.

~~~

See this photo. That's Dad in his business suit. He and my pretty mother are surrounded by my brothers, my sisters, and me. Dad liked to gather his family together for group photos. However, I'm not sure we were ever a family. The photo does not lie, but it's only a moment in time. The unfolding years would tell a different story, not this one of health, contentment, and amicability. The truth of a person's mind and heart cannot be captured in photos.

~~~

Like my mother, I'm a big fan of the television show *Law & Order*. I like the satisfaction that, most of the time, they figure out the crime, catch the criminal, and bring him or her to justice—all within 60 minutes. If I could get my brothers on a witness stand, I'd ask them to swear to tell the whole truth, like in a courtroom scene, and ask them these questions:

- When did you first become aware that Dad treated the boys differently from the girls?
- To what degree were you aware?
- What did you think about this? Did you think this was fair?
- Did you consider how your sisters might feel?
- Did you consider saying something?
- Did you take any action at all?
- If you remained silent, did you realize your silence made you complicit in perpetrating this injustice against your sisters?

~~~

Revision is the heart and soul of writing. Good writing doesn't just happen. The work of writing happens in revision, as many times as needed.

Families don't just happen either. Blood is not enough. As a family, we've had our good moments. Sharing memories of both fondness and strife, is this enough? We seem to lack something. Something happened to my brothers—the ones I cried for when my father yelled at and humiliated them with thundering words, the ones who helped sneak me into the locked and fenced playground where I played on the swings.

Something happened. I don't know what. Did they really believe we sisters were inferior to them? Was it a sense of entitlement they learned to expect as favored sons? Did this poison any compassion they might have had for their sisters and mother? Did my father's treatment of females in the family disease their hearts?

I do know we didn't learn to talk to each other, to really communicate and listen. It's easy to let old hurts pile up. New ones inevitably proliferate, whether intended or not, until they construct walls. I too am guilty of such behavior. I want communication, but don't know how to start, don't know if anyone will listen or will want to listen. My desires and actions are not always congruent, as much as I wish they were. And what I want does not seem safe. Although I want to trust my siblings, betrayal and hurt have been too common. I'm sure I have failed in their eyes too. And so we are lost to each other. Blood is not enough. Or maybe it's too much; we bloody each other too easily and it's safer and easier to stay away.

I've never told anyone in my family about being raped. It's not a topic that would arise in our infrequent meetings. I'm not sure what they would say.

Perhaps I'm more afraid that they would not hear me, that they would try to invalidate what happened, that they would not believe me.

Since leaving home, I have experienced more kindness from people unrelated to me than from my birth family. A boss who took up a collection to pay for my airfare to Honolulu when my father died. The women who welcomed me into their women's circle as a peer and continued to treat me as an equal. Friends who always make a place for me at their holiday tables. The application committee at Hedgebrook who believed in me and awarded me a highly-desirable residency at their writing retreat. My sister writers who listen closely to my words and urge me to tell my stories, who tell me the truth so I can succeed in being the best writer I can be.

And so, I have built new family here in Seattle. This is chosen family—people I choose for reasons of the heart. I've been mobile over the years living in different cities, but wherever I live, I find supportive, trustworthy people around me; this is essential to my well-being. We may not share the same blood and genes, but we talk with each other. Frequently. We share our lives and hearts. We spend time together. We listen. We know each other from the inside out, having shared secrets and stories over years and decades. Laughing and crying together. Maybe not daily, but often. These are the people I depend on when I need an ear, a shoulder, a hand; where I can find warm hearts when life turns harsh and wintry.

These people are my intentional family—my true brothers and sisters. They make home possible for me here in Seattle.

Chapter 17:
Hot Spots

The land is love. Love is what we fear. To disengage
from the earth is our own oppression
　　　　　　　　　　　　　　—Terry Tempest Williams

At the bottom of the Pacific Ocean a bit south of Hawai'i Island, magma continues to flow out of a hot spot. It's been flowing since the first island in the Hawaiian Archipelago became visible on the ocean's surface, approximately 70 million years ago. When this magma or molten rock meets the cold salt water, the reaction produces hydrothermal vents. Although the water doesn't boil due to the extreme pressure at the bottom of the ocean, the temperature of the water can reach over 700 degrees Fahrenheit. Slowly over many thousands of years, a small mound of rock forms, which becomes a taller seamount as the never-ending magma continues to travel from the earth's core to the ocean floor. Eventually this seamount rises above the ocean and becomes an island with active volcanoes, whose eruptions and lava flows create more land.

Each of the Hawaiian Islands was birthed at this hot spot and slowly drifted northwest in the direction that the Pacific tectonic plate shifts, thus making room for the creation of a new island. Hawai'i Island is the youngest of the visible islands in this chain, less than one million years old. However, another one is already forming under the ocean. Geologists have named it Lo'ihi.

Even as a new island is forming, the island of Hawai'i remains connected to the hot spot, as evidenced by current activity on Kīlauea and eruptions on Mauna Loa in the twentieth century. Mauna is the Hawaiian word for mountain. Mauna Kea and Mauna Loa are two of five volcanoes that form the island of Hawai'i. The others are Kohala, Hualālai, and Kīlauea.

Mauna Loa is the world's biggest mountain; it rises 56,000 feet from the ocean floor. While its visible height is 13,677 feet, its volume measures over

18,000 cubic miles. It is massive compared to Mount Shasta's 80 cubic miles, the largest volcano in the Cascade Range.

The islands where I grew up are not what I thought islands were—floating and disconnected from anything else. They are really the tips of massive underwater mountains. The visible mountains I so love, the volcanoes I so revere, are insignificant compared to what lies hidden below the surface.

And consider this: The word mauna (mountain) has only one more letter than mana (power, energy).

~~~

Emotional hot spots also lie below the surface. Trauma such as rape lives in the body, whether the person has knowledge of it or not. It's an energetic point that has no specific locus—an invisible wound that can impact a person's behavior, decision-making, sense of identity. As a rape survivor, I have become aware it's there when I least expect it. Even decades after the trauma, even after years of therapy dealing with the trauma, the hot spot remains active.

Physical or emotional trauma is not one event or a series of events. It is ongoing. It lives under the skin. It often changes the course of a person's life without his or her conscious consent. I speak from experience.

~~~

My journey has removed me from the islands of my birth, from my family of origin. The years have taught me what's important: to grow and to learn. The lessons are not always easy. And even though I am a transplanted islander, that is, uprooted and removed, I take comfort in knowing I am still keiki o ka ʻāina, a child of the land.

Growing up in Honolulu, I ate the fruits growing in our yard: mangoes, star fruit, and lichee. I ate local fruits and vegetables raised by others: taro and its product poi, a variety of avocados, and Mānoa lettuce, as well as island-raised beef, pork, and chicken. The land nurtured me as did the ocean: mahimahi, ʻopihi, ono, ʻahi, and aku—many kinds of fish and shellfish; also a variety of limu and other sea vegetables.

Every day I inhaled the sweet air, ate the bounty from the rich volcanic soil, and drank the water filtered by the mountains. The islands nourished the flesh and bones of this growing child. Particles of the island still reside in me, and sometimes I hear the island calling to me here in Seattle where I live. It's a physical sensation confirming my body's connection to the land, to the 'āina.

Sometimes
I feel like an island.
I land. I equals land.
Isolated yet connected.
Below the surface lies power and mass.
Massive creativity. A volcano.

No matter what my name is, how I look, what labels or categories assign themselves to me, where I live, what group claims or disclaims me, I am still and forever keiki o ka 'āina.

Chapter 18:
Parents

The world breaks everyone and afterward many are strong at the broken places.
—Ernest Hemingway

In 2011, I rear-ended a green Subaru SUV. I was following it on Lake Washington Boulevard across Madison near the Arboretum when it stopped abruptly. Even though it had the right of way, it stopped when another car appeared from a side street. I hit the brake, but no use. My body lurched forward on the impact. Damn! I had never hit another car before. Thankfully it was a bump, not a crash. There was no visible damage to either car. Still, I was shaken enough to dislodge a feeling of utter frustration. We got out of our cars and exchanged information. I called my insurance company to report the accident and was relieved when they said they would handle it.

While driving away from the accident, I reminded myself: I'm a good driver. I am careful. This accident doesn't make me a bad person. Then my mind floated to how careful I am when I take care of my friend's toddler. My friend is a single mother, and I volunteered to stay with her and help out during that first tender week after childbirth. Several months later when I needed a place to live, she invited me to move in with them. I held her son as a newborn infant, witnessed his development in awe. At this moment, he was nearly two. An adorable, intelligent child, he and I share a special bond. When he was an infant and seemed so fragile, I realized what a huge responsibility it is to take care of someone's baby and young children. Bad things can happen in a flash, like hitting this car. Or the earth cracking open a new vent to release fresh lava, like blood from a wound.

Menopause was a defining moment. I crossed over without ever being pregnant. My body changed from potential mom to barren woman. I always thought I would re-marry and have children some day; a stable and loving partner and the financial means to raise children were prerequisites. I never wanted to be in a position where I could afford something for one child and not the other. Without the urgent biological call to motherhood that some women feel, I never considered being a single mom. Parenting seemed like the most important job anyone could have—challenging enough for two adults like my own parents.

I did not consciously choose a childless life. I just never met the right guy to be a husband to me and a father to my children. Tides rose and fell. Men came and went. Some were definitely short-term, a few were serious contenders; I was heart-broken when these relationships ended. In retrospect, I feel fortunate: Long-term likely would not have worked with these men. I was still falling in love too easily and for the wrong reasons.

After driving away from the accident, I was still very emotional and thinking about my friend's son and the unpredictable things in life, things that can go wrong. A new realization sideswiped me: *I didn't have children because I knew I could not protect them from being harmed.* Like my parents did not protect me from being raped.

Omigod!

Omigod!

I had difficulty breathing, so I pulled over and parked the car.

They never knew I had been raped. No one did. I didn't tell and I forgot about it until the memories returned when I was married.

Such presumption. Having children requires such presumption, conscious or not, that they, the parents, can provide for their children, that they have the wisdom or whatever it takes to guide a soul through life, through moments of hopelessness and danger, that no matter what the adversity, they will manage. Such shining hope.

Of course, no parent can be at their child's side every minute. Even if it were possible, bad things happen that are beyond anyone's control: natural disasters, random violence, disease, wars. Subconsciously, I had decided I could not take the chance; I did not want the responsibility for a child's well-being if there was even a remote chance for harm. An irrational fear, it was also an emotional and unconscious decision arising from my own hurt and confusion as a child. The rape should not have happened. My parents were not paying attention to me, my well-being. In their negligence, they did not foresee such a crime happening in their home; it was a crime based on their failure to recognize that not all adults can be trusted with children.

How different would my life have been if I had not been raped? If I had experienced safety and protection in my home? If I had confidence that adults can protect me from egregious harm?

My mind could not recognize that children *are* resilient. That all parents make all kinds of mistakes. That people don't fully realize what parenting involves until they become parents. They don't appreciate the challenges of growing and curious children, even those of adult children. I failed to recognize that *we all learn from our mistakes*, that becoming parents is a prayer of hope and an act of abiding faith in the future.

I sat in my parked car. In shock. I let the sorrow fill me. A heaviness stayed in my body until it hurt so much that I cried. Such fear had lived inside me all these years and prevented me from having a child like my friend's darling boy.

The tears came. Gasping for air, I wept. And wept. For my little girl-self, who trusted the adults in her world. For the woman who lost her chance of being a mother. For the loss of those never-to-be babies.

~~~

The rape does not live continuously in my conscious mind or in my conscious life. I rarely think about it and years can lapse before something jogs it into my awareness. This car accident revealed that my life was bound by an invisible electric fence; I would get zapped if I explored beyond the boundaries defined by the rape. I lived my life thinking I had a range of choices when, in fact, my choices were corralled by my childhood trauma. Or did my suppressed fear and rage pre-empt the possibility of having children? The unconscious workings of my mind still hold mysteries. Irreversible consequences and unconscious decisions can surface decades later. Or not.

~~~

The lava never sleeps. Whether flowing unseen underground or under the ocean, it continues to go where it will, unexpected and dramatic when it reaches the surface, often earth-shaking and earth-changing, an unstoppable natural force burning a path of both destruction and creation. It is beautiful to behold. Mesmerizing in its power. When visible, the lava appears in stark contrast against dark, old lava fields: bright ribbons or glowing pools of fire in layers of reds, oranges, yellows. Green plants in its path are immediately incinerated; any moisture, vaporized. A black skin starts to harden on the surface and soon becomes a shell that hides the molten lava as it continues its path. This lava tube might look like solid rock, but it's not. Park rangers rope off sections of lava fields for safety from areas that could crumble under human weight.

~~~

Like verbs, crimes can be active or passive. Both action and inaction can cause pain, harm, grief. Quiet crimes occur in most families, most relationships. They may be crimes of the heart, like jealousy or lack of compassion. Crimes of selfishness or avarice. Crimes of negligence or silence, when words would make a difference. Quiet crimes are those often overlooked, not talked about, not questioned—those not dramatic enough for television, not urgent enough to warrant an ambulance. Like a child being raped by an adult's indecent touching—who would know or notice?

Emotional abuse presents another kind of quiet crime, more difficult to recognize, more subtle. Only as an adult do I recognize this and can name it. Which was worse for me: the rape, or my father's daily emotional abuse? Preferential behavior toward my brothers fell like blows on my female body and mind. Both kinds of abuse shaped me. Both live in me and color my world.

Who knows? Perhaps if I had had more confidence as a ten-year-old, I would have reacted by yelling out to my rapist, "*Stop!*" "*Help!*" and run to my parents. That would have created a scene, a confrontation, a different sort of defining moment. What I'm saying is that for this to be possible, my parents would have had to be different people—people who would believe a child, who had the patience to try to understand my attempt to tell them what happened without the proper vocabulary, who could confront this predator even though it would make everyone extremely uncomfortable, and who could reassure me that I was blameless, that I had done nothing wrong. They would have had to be people who could deal with a sordid world without averting their eyes. But they were who they were—people uncomfortable with conflict, who could not acknowledge, much less discuss it. Consequently, I was a child sexually traumatized in her home. And so, there was no scene—just another quiet crime.

I became accustomed to controlling my emotions and withdrawing instead of making a scene.

~~~

I met my worst-ever boyfriend when I lived in Vancouver, B.C. That would be Roy. Such a charmer and good dancer. Just like that, he captured my heart.

We broke up when I moved to New Mexico in 1985, but I could not forget him. I wrote letters to him like someone deranged, declaring my undying love. Ten months after arriving in Albuquerque, I was ready to move back to the Northwest. I asked him to meet me in Seattle. He did and the magic was still there. He dissolved his current relationship and we rekindled ours despite the long-distance commute. I drove north on I-5 to Vancouver, B.C., on some weekends or he came south to Seattle. For well over a year, we met like this. We were happy. I thought we were happy.

One day I surprised him when he returned from a California trip. I showed up at his place, a high-rise apartment overlooking English Bay. I had missed him and knew without a doubt he would be eager to see me.

I knocked on the door. I had my bags ready to stay for a couple of nights. His roommate greeted me and called Roy. He was not his usual upbeat, sweet self. He looked under the weather, a little haggard even. No energy. No radiant smile. I was disappointed, but thought he was tired from his flight.

"Sweetheart, how was your trip? Did you have a good time? What did you do?" I wanted to hear all about it as we sat in the living room. I was really into him, willing to overlook his lukewarm greeting and tepid kiss.

"Uh, it was good. Hung out at the beach...did a little shopping..." It was obvious that he didn't want to talk. I was puzzled, though not concerned. I went to put my things in his bedroom. I was a little tired too after the nearly three-hour drive from Seattle. Maybe we needed to make love, and all would be fine. He was always ready for that.

"Hey, I'm going to take a shower and go to bed. Come join me when you're ready." The water felt refreshing and I hoped he would join me in the shower. He didn't. I toweled off and slipped between the sheets. Later at some point, he came to bed. I snuggled close to him, pressed my body against his and felt his erection. We were good at foreplay and knew each other's bodies well, letting our hands and mouths roam freely and tenderly to those sensitive points that took us beyond the edge of excitement. Usually, we would talk and whisper endearments between our moans.

That night, Roy climbed on top of me. I opened my body to him. He entered and started pumping. He was like a stranger—or maybe worse, a zombie. Dead emotionally. No kisses, no endearments, no talking. Just mechanical thrusts hammering into me until he climaxed. He withdrew, turned over, and went to sleep. I had wanted him, but not like this. Why did it feel so awful? At one point, I wanted to shove him away and tell him, "Get off me! What the hell do you think you're doing?" This was not loving, not pleasure. I lay there in shock, wondering what was wrong, if I had done something wrong.

The next morning, he rose before me and got dressed. When I joined him in the kitchen, he could not look at me. His lips were a tight line, a hyphen across his face. Before I could say anything, he spoke. A cold stone speaking.

"Loreen, I've met someone else. She's a flight attendant and I went to meet her in Los Angeles. I want to be with her."

The callousness. The utter callousness of his words stunned me. They were torpedoes slamming into me. They scattered my molecules, sent them flying. I felt dizzy. Like I could vaporize. Poof! Clearly I was nothing to him and I wished I could beam myself away, be anywhere but here. Incredibly, my body remained rooted. Immobilized. *I have to get out of here. Have to!* Somehow, I gathered myself together, got my things, and left. No scene.

No "What the fuck do you mean?" No "You cowardly prick, you could have told me this when I arrived!" No "I hate you!" No kicking or punching or scratching. No hitting him with something that would bloody him.

When I got in the car and drove away, the pain hit. It seared me to the core and brought tears—such a deluge that it was a wonder I could drive at all. When the rage surfaced, it was a killing rage that would have turned me into a murderer if I'd had a gun.

For weeks I was shaky, unstable like a chemical compound that changes form: liquid, solid, gas.

Glass. I was glass shattered into a thousand little pieces, irreconcilable to wholeness. Shards sharp enough to cut flesh, make it bleed. I raged. How could he treat me like this? Had he ever even loved me? Now I hated him. I hated myself for being so fragile, so easily destroyed.

Waterfall. A continuous cascade of tears. Endless tears. So much water, enough to drown in. Death looked appealing, but I wasn't suicidal. Depressed, yes. A dark puddle that no light could penetrate. Devoid of movement. Static.

Shadow. I felt one-dimensional, skimming along the surface of my days. Another mutation: I became a wraith. I defied gravity and flew into the skies across the miles. I hunted Roy. I wanted to invade his dreams, inflict hurt, illness, sleeplessness, drive him over the brink.

I flitted from one form to another as my emotions surfaced and shifted.

I considered voodoo dolls. I fantasized about bombs. About finding some goon to break Roy's fingers or pummel his depraved body. Thoughts of revenge became my drug of choice, filling me with new purpose. Like the plague, he needed to be stopped. Maybe a hit man. Uh-uh. No, he deserved to die slowly. Painfully.

I'm not proud of these murderous thoughts. It was a dark time. Very dark. I felt lost, irretrievably lost. Months went by. The days blended together. My job kept me sane. I was productive and responsible as an admin assistant at the lens manufacturing company. This was something I could count on, something I knew I was good at. Something that provided distraction from the torture of self-doubt and the unknowable.

How long had he been cheating on me? If I had not shown up when I did, how long was he planning to string me along? My living in another city made it so convenient for his schemes of infidelity and his playboy fantasies. And me with stars in my eyes, none the wiser.

We had shared almost four years together before New Mexico and after. We had lived together for part of this time. Besides my former husband, he was the only other man I had lived with. We were talking about living in the same city again. He even mentioned the possibility of moving to Seattle. I committed everything to our relationship. It was not a passing thing. It was as serious as fire. Nothing dubious about fire. Fire has no ambiguity.

The ugly truth inflamed me. If he had loved me, how could he treat me like this? He casually threw me to the curb like yesterday's garbage. Of course, the clues had been there. I remember when *Cats* was playing in Vancouver, I wanted to go and asked if we could get tickets. No, we couldn't go. I don't even remember what reason he gave. I was disappointed, but let it go. One weekend when I was at his place, I saw torn ticket stubs from the play on his dresser. I didn't question him. I still wanted to believe he truly loved me and wasn't a first-class liar and bastard. Such a fool!

I wondered if he was capable of loving women—how many had he infected over the years? I should not have been surprised. I knew he was a serial monogamist of the worst kind, unable to be without a steady woman. He always found a replacement before leaving his current relationship; he had started shopping for a new girlfriend before I left the city. I was stupid enough to think he would be different with me.

I've had my share of broken hearts over the years. I've likely broken a few along the way. But here's the truth: My heart was broken a long time ago by Dad, who always saw and treated me differently from my brothers. What I perceived as a lack of love from my father has influenced my choice in men. It's influenced my self-image and sense of what I deserve.

When I started writing the stories I wasn't supposed to tell, I thought the rape was a defining moment for the memoir. It was and it wasn't. What became more apparent, more damaging, was the prevailing family environment—the suppression of female voices and value, the hoarding of words and affection, the absence of safety. These set the stage for the rape. This is not blame, it's a fact that has become apparent to me only with time.

Presence can be absence: While physically present in my growing-up years, Dad was emotionally absent. Completely not available.

~~~

As an adult, I struggle to understand my parents. What events might have shaped their lives?

In a sense, both Mom and Dad had been orphans. From the day she was born, Mom had no control over her life and destiny. All major decisions were made by men: First, her birth father decided she was to be adopted out, then her adoptive father held authority over her life. Later when she married, her husband held the power.

Dad was an only child. When the family reunited in Honolulu, he was 11 and six siblings were in his future. His early years in China were fatherless since his father was away in Honolulu establishing a new life. I wonder if other children in his village also had absent fathers or whether he was singled out by his loss. I wonder if his father ever visited when he was growing up or if he was a complete stranger when Dad, as a boy, stepped off the *Steamship China* in Honolulu Harbor and met him.

Mom lived a privileged life compared to her birth siblings. Her adoptive parents doted on her and they lived comfortably. She understood and did not question her position as a daughter and later as wife and mother. She knew she was adopted and met her birth parents and siblings. She must have noticed the relative prosperity of her adoptive family compared to her struggling birth parents. I often wonder how she felt about her circumstances. Did she harbor any anger or resentment? Did she ever feel confusion about where she belonged or where she owed her loyalty? She never talked about these things. Mom looked at life as a glass half-full and so lived in grace as much as anyone can. It's possible that she might have felt lucky to have two families.

I wonder if Mom's impoverished birth was known to my Dad's sisters and whether this factored into their disdain toward her, their feelings of superiority. At some point after Dad's death, Mom confided that she had asked Dad to speak to his sisters about their behavior toward her. He did not. He failed to support his wife. Not only would this have been the decent thing to do, but also it would have supported her traditional and substantial role as the eldest brother's wife. Mom did not expect them to kowtow to her; she just wanted them to stop sniping at her.

When Dad confided to me about his disappointment in my three brothers becoming teachers, I admit I was relieved to not be the target of his displeasure...this time. I was also wary since he never spoke directly to those who displeased him. He would tell others and let them carry the news to the guilty ones. It's no mystery why we siblings have communication problems.

And so, as traditional as Dad was, as offended as he was when my brothers' teachers usurped *his* traditional role and persuaded my brothers to pursue teaching careers, he took no action to reinforce Mom's traditional role in the family hierarchy in the early years of their marriage, to make Mom's life easier regarding her sisters-in-law.

Life is not often black and white, so I try to understand what might have motivated the aunties' behavior. Perhaps they begrudged the fact that Dad would inherit everything from Po Po when Po Po died. That my mother and her children would share this wealth that *their* father had acquired. They could say nothing. They could do nothing. Neither did they temper their feelings. They continued to honor my father as their eldest brother while transferring their anger to Mom.

To be sure, Dad had earned their respect when he became head of the Lee family after Gung Gung died. When he took over the family business, the store in Chinatown, and the family finances, I can only imagine the shock he must have felt in discovering the massive debt that his father had left behind. Dad had been working in the store as Gung Gung's right hand, but apparently, he wasn't privy to everything, particularly not the complete financial picture. As a dutiful son, Dad bore the full weight of this responsibility, working long and hard to repay his father's debt. He had to. There was no one else, no other option. Although Dad's siblings knew he was in charge, they may not have known what he had to do to ensure their lives and lifestyle were not disrupted when their father died.

~~~

Dad loved me the best way he knew how. He did not know that his masseur, this seemingly unassuming Japanese man was a pedophile. Mr. Kishi—I don't know his first name, I don't know his story. In earlier versions of writing about this, he remained unnamed. Then I thought "Mr. K." would suffice until a writing instructor questioned whether this was self-censorship. Was I silencing myself again?

Naming my abuser is important.

I remember.

It's important to tell what happened.

And who did what.

Dad did not realize how strong-willed I was, how I chafed under his control and prejudice. Nor did he realize that I would dare to defy him and plan my escape by whatever means available. That an unconscious, lava-like anger burned inside me. Did he ever wonder how his favoritism might affect his daughters? Probably not. He never second-guessed his decisions and behavior as I learned to do. Feeling diminished, I often doubted myself. I, who was less loved and less important; what did I know?

Dad wasn't perfect, but he provided for all of us in his large family. His earnings paid for the comfort of our home, all food, medical needs, books and education, shoes and clothing, everyday household items, magazine subscriptions, water and utilities, bus fare and automobile expenses, property taxes, my sewing classes, my sister's piano and ballet lessons, our toys—everything we needed.

He wanted his sons to have careers with good salaries so they could provide well for their families and help him and Mom in their twilight years. He gave financial support when his sons purchased their homes. The husbands of my married sisters received no help from Dad because, according to Chinese tradition, it was the responsibility of the husbands' parents to help their sons. I had chosen divorce and had no husband; since I did not remarry, I was on my own. Standing alone. As usual.

Dad enjoyed children. I observed this not within our immediate family, but when he interacted with other children, like my younger cousins. He spoke playfully to them. It was startling to see this side of him, and I admit to feeling jealous. Why didn't he talk to us this way?

And yet his aloofness did not mean he didn't care. It's likely he was often exhausted by the responsibilities of work and the demands of his large family. He was an older father, nearly fifty when I was born. I am awed by his tremendous confidence to marry late in life and to quickly father so many children: six by his early fifties.

His priorities and those of his children were often incompatible. Christmas Day is a good example. We weren't a Christian family. We celebrated this holiday in a secular way as many good American families did. It was an exciting time for me and my siblings. Dad brought home a Christmas tree, often a poor scraggly one, dry from its long journey by boat from the Pacific Northwest. Still, we joyfully decorated it with lights and ornaments. With good food, presents aplenty, lots of candies and cookies, there was much to look forward to at Christmastime.

I got up early on Christmas morning, anxious to start opening presents. And with six children, presents overflowed beneath the Christmas tree. But, no, I learned to rein in my excitement while waiting for everyone else to get up, especially for Dad to set up his camera and get us all arranged around the tree for the annual Christmas photo. With a child's impatience, it seemed like hours before the photos were taken. By the time we got to the presents, most of my excitement had fizzled away. This became our holiday tradition: often a funny-looking Christmas tree and waiting for Dad, the photographer. It was so important to Dad to record his family with all the presents under the colored lights and ornaments. Looking closer at these photos, I see children looking distracted, perhaps pissed off. And Dad never got into the photos. He was the photographer and could have used a timer to join us. Instead, Dad is absent from the family Christmas photos.

After my divorce, my parents invited me over for dinner once a week or more. Sometimes other family members joined us. One evening, it was just me and my parents. The meal was pleasant but not memorable. What impressed me was that Dad kept putting food on my plate, encouraging me to eat. When we had dinner guests, Dad always made sure there was plenty of food and urged our guests to have more of everything. I have a good appetite so I didn't need much coaxing. When I left, they gave me some leftovers and other food to take home with me, as was their custom. When I got home and was putting the food away, I realized this food was Dad's expression of love for me. This was his most direct expression of love, his most comfortable way of showing his love. I finally had tangible proof. I finally understood.

My parents loved me. I know this for sure even though they did not express their love in ways that were obvious or would have made sense to me.

I needed the language of affection, the silent words felt on the skin.

Ultimately, I love my parents, flaws and all. They made mistakes. They committed quiet crimes. I have come to recognize the complexity of our lives, singly and together, how they have impacted and influenced me and my life. And I know they loved me, even during those times I surely caused them anguish and sleepless nights. Parenting is not for the weak or weak-hearted. They loved me even though they didn't understand my choices and perhaps disagreed with them. Even when I doubted their love, the love was there. They tried their best to show that loving someone means accepting the whole person, all the good and the bad, all the pain and the joy.

In a brazen mood, I once asked my mother why they had had so many children, not that I believed my parents ever discussed having a large family, but surely after four children with three sons to ensure the lineage and well-being of the family, most adults would have stopped making babies.

She said, "I had no problems. Being pregnant or giving birth. No complications." Everything happened so easily that she never questioned that her life should be otherwise.

And what about the pain of giving birth? She didn't deny it, but the physical pain is quickly forgotten. "It's like amnesia," she told me. With the joy of having a new baby and the many maternal demands, the pain recedes into a distant memory. I suppose this is nature's way of ensuring propagation. I also think Mom took genuine pleasure in having her babies. This was her job and her worth as a Chinese woman.

I credit my mother for my love of books and reading, a fondness for words, libraries, and librarians. Mom took us to the public library even before I could read. I loved the library, with its unlimited choices.

Dad also gave me something precious. He taught me the meaning and importance of having good friends. Throughout his lifetime, he kept his boyhood friends; we often piled in the car on Sundays to visit them all over the island. I met them as older men on these visits, but I recognized their faces from old black-and-white photos: the handsome young men with my dad. In a house full of sisters, Dad needed his guy friends and they bonded like brothers—going to the beach, playing tennis, taking excursions, and coming over to the Lee house for dinner.

Dad also named us. He gave us both American and Chinese names. The last time I used my Chinese name was in Chinese school where I was known as Lee Lilyn. Family name first.

Becoming a writer, I decided to use my entire name, including my Chinese name. Loreen Lilyn Lee. I liked the sound of it, the alliteration. Other women with this Chinese name often spell it Lai Lin. My father decided to be creative in his spelling. Although I knew the name referred to a flower, I didn't know which one. I woke one day at a writing retreat at Hedgebrook and noticed the day lilies in the stained glass-window in my cottage. It was a eureka moment. The spelling of my name Lilyn embodies the name of the flower.

Mah jongg is another link to my mother. I've been playing mah jongg with my Asian American gal friends for twenty-plus years now. My mother enjoyed playing, and she taught me this game when I was a child. It's brought me many hours of pleasure and deepened friendships with other Asian American women. In any Chinatown, one often hears the clicking of the mah jongg tiles being washed, or mixed up. It's a comforting sound that makes me happy to be Chinese.

I learned t'ai chi and qigong. Dad used to practice t'ai chi every morning and every evening. I wonder if watching him gave me an advantage, some kind of body memory, in learning these ancient movements. When I attended a two-week t'ai chi retreat in China in 2008, I had lessons nearly every day outdoors among rows of gnarly pine trees in a qi field of sandy dirt. Their twisted trunks looked human, seemed to instruct me and the other students to bend, but stay rooted.

I loved being in China. I didn't speak the language and couldn't read the signs but seeing calligraphy everywhere and being among people who could have been related to me, I felt my body ease right into the scene like indulging in a comforting memory. It was a whole-body sensation, both tingling with excitement and relaxed at the same time. I felt at home although I was clearly a foreigner. In one temple, a woman started talking to me in Mandarin. When I got someone to explain that I was American and did not speak Chinese, she was incredulous. It was outside of her reality, beyond her comprehension. How was it possible that a Chinese person did not speak Chinese? Still, she had recognized me as one of her people.

China is the land of my ancestors. This is where my father was born, and I gained insight about him on this visit—a visceral learning. He was thoroughly Chinese. He was the family patriarch. He was the giver of names. Cantonese was his first language and he spoke two other dialects. His world in Chinatown kept him linked to the old country and culture; it validated his Chinese-ness. Being in China gave me a peek into why Chinese people have such pride, even a sense of superiority. It's not only the longevity of the culture unlike any other. It's the wisdom expressed in yin yang, the importance of striving for balance. It's the richness and the aesthetics of the culture, expressed in its sumptuous cuisine, the attention to fine detail in the arts and architecture. I was enraptured by the colors, bright primary colors, and artistry applied in painting the beams of the covered walkway at the Summer Palace, those inside the roofs of pavilions and over doorways. It's the importance of and connection to nature evidenced in city parks, the temples built out over the water or at seemingly impossible elevations in the mountains.

When I visited the Forbidden City and the Great Wall I was awed by their grand scale, how someone had the capacity to imagine something so immense, much less construct it. When I saw the Grand Canyon, I had a feeling in my body I was unprepared for. I knew it would be stunning, but it was more, much more. Standing at the lookout, I felt the sacredness of that place. I took a few moments to be silent, as if I was in a cathedral, to absorb the grandness and beauty of the landscape, its layers of earthen shades. That broken place where the earth was cleaved felt so alive, both elemental and symbolic. In China, I felt again a sense of the Divine, this time as expressed through human genius.

Perhaps the older I get, the more Chinese I become.

~~~

Despite Mom's powerlessness in her marriage, I admire and honor her. I'm sure she did not always agree with her husband, but she was a woman of her time. She persevered and lived the role of a traditional wife and mother. Until she didn't.

She broke tradition by supporting her daughters against male privilege.

She broke tradition by taking a stand against the terms of Dad's will and my brother's willfulness.

She broke tradition by forcing the equal distribution of Dad's estate to all seven of us and overturning Dad's consistent and pernicious favoritism of my brothers.

In effect, she rose up and shouted, *"Enough!"* She could not have said or done this while Dad was alive, but he was gone and she decided she could do this brave thing; she could move off the path worn deeply into the ground by years and years of following Chinese tradition and staying silent. Her action could not undo years of emotional abuse to herself and her children, but it was an expression of power nonetheless.

I never wanted the kind of marriage my mother had: material comfort with unfulfilled emotional needs; an unequal partnership. When they married, he was nearly old enough to be her father, and he treated her like a child. I can't pretend I knew my parents very well as individuals, people in their own right, but I witnessed some of their interactions and decided this scenario of the powerless wife and the all-powerful husband was not what I wanted.

Mom surprised me. While Dad remained intractable to the end, the classic example of a Chinese husband and father, Mom proved her strength—the strength of a mother's love for all her children. By overturning her traditional role, she transformed and became my hero. She rose up into a mountain.

~~~

The lava never sleeps. It burns with intense heat. Afire. Aglow. Pele makes no explanation for what she does or doesn't do nor offers apologies. She is all passion and fire, at times explosive. She fiercely stands up for herself and holds her ground against those who would destroy her.

Legends tell about the rivalry between Pele and her sister Namakaokaha'i of the Sea. When Pele first arrived in the Hawaiian Islands, she looked for a home where the sacred fires could be safely stored in a deep pit. Her sister kept drowning out each pit time after time, island after island, until Pele made her home on Mauna Loa on the Big Island. Here she found safety.

Sibling stuff. I can relate.

~~~

The lava never sleeps. Neither does the love. My mother chose to love all her children equally. I also choose love. Ever-flowing. Aloha. I choose life. Because a life without love is the ultimate crime.

Chapter 19:
Gifts

*My connection to the natural world is my connection
to self—erotic, mysterious, and whole.*
                    —Terry Tempest Williams

A moment in May. The year is 1995. I am aboard *Hawai'iloa,* a fifty-seven-foot double-hulled canoe, the second one of its kind built to replicate the great Polynesian voyaging canoes of long ago. Sailing throughout the Pacific for untold centuries, these canoes transported people navigating unfamiliar waters with no instruments, only their native intelligence of the natural elements—stars, wind, and waves. In fact, only a few weeks earlier this canoe had completed its maiden voyage to the Marquesas Islands, located twenty-four hundred miles southeast from Hawai'i.

In many ways I too had recently completed an arduous journey. At the age of forty-six, I finally finished the requirements for a bachelor's degree. The years of both working and going to school had teemed with uncertainty, with no visible shoreline offering a reference point for solid ground. Now in this vessel, surrounded by native Hawaiians, Polynesians, and others born and raised in Hawai'i, I am comforted by the varying shades of brown and by the sounds of island voices speaking the local lingo: "Eh, howzit?" An easy camaraderie both familiar and genuinely warm resides in the canoe even though I met most of these people only an hour or two ago.

Someone blows a conch shell, pū. The sound resonates between water and sky to announce the canoe's singular presence, a small sailing vessel clearly from another time, to all onlookers on the shore and in other boats. My body shivers with excitement as the canoe glides easily over the waters.

However, these are not Hawaiian waters. We are riding the waters of Puget Sound in Washington state.

~~~

As a child, I was captivated by an adventure story. In 1947, Thor Heyerdahl, a Norwegian explorer and archaeologist, sailed a raft that he named *Kon-Tiki* across the Pacific from Peru. His goal: to demonstrate that ancient people from South America could have settled Polynesia. It was a bold idea at the time, and his successful journey seemed to provide a possible answer. Still, it was not conclusive, so I continued to be intrigued by the mystery surrounding Polynesians.

Who are the Polynesians? Where did they come from? How was it possible for these Polynesian people to inhabit Pacific islands scattered over ten million miles of ocean? Was it by accident? How could a culture with no navigational tools, no metal to build powerful vessels, and no canvas for sails possibly have reached so many islands? And how was it even possible to sail from west to east against the prevailing winds and currents?

Recent archaeological and linguistic evidence indicate that the Polynesians originated in Southeast Asia. In fact, canoe paddles as old as seven thousand years old have been discovered in southeast China along the coast between Hong Kong and Shanghai. Could this ancient seafaring culture prove to be the ancestors of the Polynesians and Hawaiians? If so, how did they migrate? The stories in ancient Polynesian chants and legends describe voyaging canoes, while petroglyphs in Hawai'i depict them. Are these accurate? Did the Polynesians practice an unknown long-distance seafaring tradition?

And so, the canoe *Hōkūle'a* was born. The vision of three men—a scientist, an artist of native Hawaiian ancestry, and a modern-day mariner—this canoe was designed and built to test the theory that ancient Polynesian seafarers did have ocean-going vessels and navigational skills, that these people had migrated from the western Pacific across thousands of miles of open water to eventually populate the Pacific Triangle marked by New Zealand, Hawai'i, and Rapa Nui (Easter Island).

The Hawaiian name for the star Arcturus, Hōkūle'a means "Star of Gladness." At its zenith, this is the guiding star in the heavens over Hawai'i. In 1976, after locating a master navigator from the Micronesian island of Satawal to join its small crew, fifteen members to Tahiti and thirteen members on the return trip, the *Hōkūle'a* completed her maiden voyage. With two hulls sixty feet long connected by an open deck similar to today's catamarans and two sails, this canoe completed a journey that confirmed ancient stories and renewed cultural pride for native peoples in Hawai'i and all over the Pacific.

Replicating an ancient canoe seemed a simple idea. In fact, it was epic. Seismic. Transformative. Star of gladness indeed. The success of *Hōkūle'a's* maiden voyage rekindled the hidden fire, the latent lava, in the hearts of both Hawaiians and local people. Here was proof of native intelligence and wisdom of Hawaiian ancestors. More than an important piece of their lineage, this proof instigated a passion for culture and traditional values that rose to the surface and burst forth in an unstoppable flow. The result was a flourishing of Hawaiian music and dance, language, poetry, spirituality, arts and crafts, and traditional values—possibly not seen since the missionaries first landed in these islands. A resurgence of native arts and cultural values swept through, not only Hawai'i, but all of Polynesia.

The Polynesian Voyaging Society in Honolulu, founded in 1973, has guided the construction of Hawai'i's traditional voyaging canoes and supported many journeys throughout the Pacific Triangle for cultural and educational purposes. A voyaging community was reborn and now thrives once again in the Pacific. *Hōkūle'a* was the spark that re-ignited this cultural fire, and her star-power burns brilliantly still.

Bringing her own inimitable fire, the Goddess Pele has returned with volcanic activity non-stop for several decades, thus demonstrating her power and glory. Her presence is impossible to ignore. Her magnificence, indisputable. Is this coincidence or something cosmic?

~~~

Several weeks before sailing on *Hawai'iloa*, I was laboring over an important speech. Friends, university staff and professors, other graduates, students, and strangers—all eyes would be on me, expecting something eloquent, profound, and possibly inspiring as the 1995 student commencement speaker for the University of Washington, Bothell. My emotions fluctuated between fireworks-like excitement and catatonic fear. I struggled with revision after revision to condense my entire baccalaureate experience at the Bothell campus into ten minutes. Slowly the speech began to emerge when I faced another dilemma.

Over the years, I came to realize how my birthplace, the Hawaiian Islands, has shaped my identity. Hawai'i was and is an integral part of my being—no matter what, I am forever connected to Hawai'i and its culture in intangible ways. But how to convey this connection on this important occasion? In true island-girl fashion, I decided to wear a maile lei to honor the occasion. And to honor the land of my birth.

I didn't know how to get a fresh lei for this event.

~~~

Living in Seattle and away from Hawai'i gave me much-needed appreciation for my birthplace. I grew hungry for the culture and visited the islands whenever possible. However, it wasn't often enough. Hawaiian music comforted my soul: I listened to CDs and went to concerts by Hawaiian musicians touring in the Seattle area. I took classes in Hawaiian quilting. And I found restaurants and stores that specialize in Hawaiian and local-style foods like poi.

"You like some poi?" How do you tell a local from a visitor? Offer some poi. While not completely foolproof, it comes pretty darn close.

Always, I've always eaten poi. Born in Honolulu, I was likely given a bowl of poi and a spoon as a toddler learning to feed myself. And I likely made a mess. Poi on my face. On the table. On my clothes. On the floor. When some got into my mouth, it tasted so good. Soft on the tongue, smooth and slippery and easy to swallow. As I got older, I was less messy, but we kids liked playing with our food. When wet poi dried on our arms and fingers, it looked like wrinkled skin. We made our hands into claws and cackled like old witches.

Raised on poi, I love it still and order it at Hawaiian-style restaurants in Seattle. I understand people's aversion if they've never had it. Made from cooked taro root, also known as taro corm or kalo, poi is gray with purple tones, or more accurately, mauve. Mixed with water, it has the consistency of cake batter, depending on how much water is added.

I watched my mother prepare poi for her hungry children. At the time, we referred to it as poi. However, it was more accurately pa'i 'ai, or mashed taro, which becomes poi when mixed with water. At home, she soaked the unopened plastic bag she'd brought home from the grocery store in a bowl of cold water to loosen the sticky contents from the sides of the bag. After a few hours, she got ready to mix the poi. Removing her rings, she turned the bag inside out and, with her hands, scraped the pa'i 'ai into a large ceramic bowl. She squeezed the bag several times to get every morsel. A soft, lumpy mass sat in the bottom of the bowl, which was in the sink so she could add cold water from the faucet a little at a time. With her hand, she dug into the mass, stirred and squeezed out the lumps, stirred and squeezed. Kneading and slapping, she worked the paʻi ʻai into poi until it was smooth. Adding water stretched the poi to feed her six children.

From the bag to my mother's hand to the table. It was a splendid ritual.

When I prepare poi, it feels good to immerse my hand into the thick mashed taro, watch it transform into a smooth "batter," cool to the touch. I perform the same movements as my mother, stirring and squeezing the poi. I don't "make" the poi, but it feels creative—a satisfying and tactile experience, as I imagine bakers must feel when they knead bread dough. When done, I kahi the bowl, wiping my hand, back and front, on the rim of the bowl, just as my mother did, then I lick any remnants of poi clinging to my fingers. The rim of the serving bowl must be clean to show respect for this food and those who will eat it.

Eating poi feeds both body and soul.

The legend of the kalo plant explains why this plant is so special to Hawaiians. Plants and ʻāina are ancestors to Hawaiians. All are part of the natural world. All are family. Long ago two deities fell in love and produced a baby boy. However, he was stillborn and his parents buried him. On his grave a shoot appeared and grew into the first kalo plant with large heart-shaped leaves. The parents named the plant Hāloa. When they gave birth to a healthy baby boy, they also named this child Hāloa, the same name given to the plant, which was considered to be their son's older brother.

Historically, Hawaiians eat poi with their fingers. I use a spoon. More texture than taste, it has a subtle flavor, rather bland. How do you describe the taste of white bread or potatoes? Same thing. And like them, poi is a staple food. It is central to Hawaiian culture and identity. I can eat poi plain, but we usually mixed in other food to add flavor. Mom fried onions with canned corned beef. Or we might have some kālua pig on the side. Or salty lomi lomi salmon or canned sardines. Fish and poi. Food from ocean and land. Really simple. Really good.

When I visit the islands, having Hawaiian food is a priority. Memory tells me it was even better before. Is this true or is nostalgia coloring my memories? Or have my taste buds changed with age? Food generally was simpler back in the middle of the twentieth century

Eating island fruits tells me my taste buds are intact. Fresh, tree-ripened papayas and mangoes sing on my tongue, bring sunshine to my insides. They are food fit for the gods—beautiful to behold, luscious and delicious, and nourishing. Of course, I never appreciated them when I was a kid. They were always available. Almost every family had a mango tree and shared their bounty. I didn't recognize how special these local fresh fruits were or how extraordinary it was to have fresh fruits year-round. Maturity and absence have expanded and deepened my appreciation. When I visit, I want to ingest the islands, fill my body with food from the land of my birth, as well as experience the islands on my skin. The warm salty ocean. Sandy beaches. Cooling trade winds. The sweet, warm air.

A growing awareness of a deep connection to these islands emerged. I found the land and culture residing in my body. Where I was born shaped me and built a foundation for me. It grounds me still. I am keiki o ka 'āina. Child of the land. This is where I am rooted and forever nurtured, internally and externally. Poi and island fruits revive bodily memories of growing up in the islands. Of days of endless sunshine and boundless energy. Of my mother preparing simple meals.

I am local and keiki o ka 'āina. However, I am not Hawaiian.

Many Californians, Hawaiians, and local people from Hawai'i have moved to Washington. Californian is a label describing where someone is from or was born and raised. Being Californian describes place and geography. However, being Hawaiian has ethnic or genetic meaning. Hawaiian people belong to the larger racial group of Polynesians or, as designated on American government forms, Pacific Islanders.

Being American is another label identifying where someone is born. More importantly, it communicates citizenship and nationality.

I am Chinese American. My ethnicity is Chinese, and I was born in Hawai'i when it was still a U.S. Territory. To describe where I was born and raised, I can say "I'm from Hawai'i."

Or "I'm Hawai'i-born."

Or "I'm a local girl from Hawai'i."

There are several options. But out of respect to Hawaiian people, I would never say "I'm Hawaiian." It's too glib, too insensitive to Hawaiians, their culture, and their history. And it's inaccurate. I'm not presuming that all Hawaiian people feel this way, but some do. I understand and honor their feelings. If non-Chinese people are born in Beijing, they would not and could not claim to be Chinese.

Native Hawaiians sometimes refer to themselves as Kanaka Maoli. This is a term that cannot be co-opted by non-Hawaiians. Kanaka means man, human being, or Hawaiian. Maoli means native, indigenous, or true.

In school, my history classes focused on American and European history. Even world history came filtered through a Western lens. Hawai'i's history was not offered. In third grade we spent about a week learning the names of Hawaiian monarchs and visited 'Iolani Palace. That was it. Even though my school, St. Andrew's Priory, was founded by Queen Emma, consort of King Kamehameha IV, we had no classes in Hawaiian history. We didn't learn anything about how Hawaiians became oppressed and marginalized in their own country; how white colonialists arrived and imposed their "superior" knowledge and religions on these natives and banned the Hawaiian language and other cultural practices.

As an adult, I sought to fill this void to better understand the history of my homeland and the events that still impact the islands today. I found many books recording this painful history, even one by the last monarch of the Kingdom of Hawai'i, Queen Lili'uokalani. Once a sovereign nation, the kingdom became a republic when white businessmen, some descendants of missionaries and citizens of the country, some not even citizens, overthrew the queen in a coup d'état to protect their own interests. They stole this kingdom, while other nations, notably the United States and Great Britain, idly stood by.

While its rightful monarch and her representatives made appeals in Washington, D.C., to restore her kingdom, these same businessmen were lobbying Congress to annex the Hawaiian Islands. Many of these businessmen, descendants of missionaries who first arrived in 1820, accrued political power over several decades through alliances and influence over the monarchy. They even had the impudence to coerce a king to implement a new constitution, which effectively shifted the balance of power, disenfranchising Hawaiians while enfranchising white landowners.

Hawaiians have lived in these islands for approximately two thousand years. The first Chinese migrated to these shores just over two hundred years ago, making the Chinese relatively newcomers. Other ethnic groups followed to work on the sugar plantations. Although new immigrants struggled to make a home here, all contributed to the cultural mix that is unique to these islands.

Gung Gung Lee landed in Honolulu in 1887. From impoverished immigrant to prominent Chinatown businessman, by the early twentieth century, he managed to buy property, build a home, and bring his wife and son, my father, from China. My grandmother bore six more children after arriving, and generations later, many of their descendants still live in Hawaiʻi. Thanks to my grandfather's hard work, we grew up local, enjoying all the bounty and beauty of the islands.

I am proud to be a local, someone born in the islands who understands the subtleties of language and labels, the sometimes tentative links between various ethnic groups and cultures residing here, and how important these groups are to the local culture and history of these islands. Local is an attitude, a mindset, a value system, a lifestyle, and ultimately a choice. Anyone can claim to be a local, but *being* local is more nuanced. Locals and non-locals may look alike, but an ocean of history and circumstances can separate them. Some hapa may look more white than Hawaiian, but they are still Hawaiian. Some recent Asian immigrants may be brownies, that is, they can blend into Hawaiʻi's tanned masses, but they have no connection to the history of non-whites in Hawaiʻi, such as the plantation culture. Likewise, some local haole are born and raised in Hawaiʻi; some come from elsewhere and take root here. There are differences. Still, all can claim to be local.

For such a small land mass, the Hawaiian Islands has an incredibly diverse population. The population here exemplifies the farthest point from homogeneity. In general, the various ethnic groups get along, not always, but mostly; living on an island makes peaceful co-existence highly desirable. This is not to say that prejudices and tensions don't exist between individuals and between various ethnic groups. Such tensions can and do arise, sometimes within the same ethnic groups. Sometimes within families. It's the human condition.

For example, my parents preferred that we marry within the Chinese community. Plain and simple. The Chinese tend to regard themselves as a superior people, and diluting the blood is frowned upon. However, because of the lack of Chinese women, many immigrant men married women of other races, including Hawaiians. These blendings of cultures often produce children of exceptional beauty.

Perhaps being local is a matter of rhythms. Hawaiʻi-born people live and are raised in the ever-present rhythms of nature. The ocean is never far away. The mountains are always visible, never-yielding. Whether green curtain or brown cinder cone, they turn the eyes skyward. Active volcanoes give Hawaiʻi's people ample proof of the earth's vitality, the power of Madame Pele. The pace of life here is slower, where island time often is not determined by clocks. Perhaps this Hawaiian-style time is necessary for gaining reverence, a proper reference, for life.

Eloquence. Flow of lava, rumbling of the earth, shifting sands, undulation of ocean, air currents translating to trade winds—nature is constantly and noticeably in motion. And with motion comes Sound. Songs. Music—a global language.

Cadence. Multiple mother tongues. A symphony of human sounds from East and West. Incoherent to one another except for Pidgin English. Whether practiced or suppressed, Pidgin is part of growing up local. It's another kind of rhythm that local ears learn and local bodies ingest, becoming attuned, like pulsations in land and ocean.

Magic. Perhaps it's something magical in the genes of those born in the islands. The Polynesians have always held special reverence for these islands, considering them sacred, having life force, mana. According to one Hawaiian elder, "The land is not sacred because the temple is here. The temple is sacred because of the land."

I like being local. No matter my age, I can call myself a local girl. Local people understand each other without a lot of words. We always ask, "What high school you went to?" It's short-hand or code to understanding the individual—more important than their neighborhood since someone going to a private school can live anywhere. A person's high school roughly identifies that person's socioeconomic background, whether she is country or townie. We locals understand Pidgin English and local jargon. For directions, if someone says, "Go ma uka," we locals understand to head toward the mountains; "Go ma kai" means head toward the ocean. We know how delicious, really 'ono, island food is.

"You like some poi?"

Big smile. "Of course!"

~~~

It's Memorial Day weekend. My friend Joan and I arrive at Golden Gardens Park near the marina at Shilshole Bay to attend a Hawaiian cultural festival honoring the voyaging canoes. We plan to stay a few hours before heading to the Folklife Festival at Seattle Center. The weather is sunny and deliciously warm. The lush music of a slack-key guitar on the audio system drifts over the sand and the Sound. The notes are like magnets pulling at my heart. The proximity to water seems to amplify my feelings of belonging and longing.

The two of us wander throughout the park not wanting to miss a single thing—a stage on one end will feature entertainment throughout the afternoon; display boards tell the story of voyaging canoes; various booths feature Hawaiian crafts, products, and food; I've already made note of the booth selling shave ice and will come back later.

Joan and I keep returning to a particular crafts booth, where I become acquainted with Dora. Joan is deciding whether to buy a basket woven from lau hala leaves while I covet the jewelry displayed—bracelets, necklaces, and earrings made from kukui nuts, coconut shell, and other Polynesian seeds. Dora is the embodiment of aloha and I'm drawn to her natural friendliness like flowers turning to the light. About five feet tall including her black hair pulled into a knot at the top of her head, she radiates a welcoming energy in her ready smile and sparkling eyes.

Dora is weaving together vines I don't recognize.

She says, "This is maile."

"Oh, I've never seen this variety. The leaves are smaller, yeah?" The fragrance is undeniable—a sweet earthiness from Hawai'i's forests.

"We sell a variety of maile lei at my lei stand at the Honolulu airport. This is maile lau li'i. In fact, I have to come back to Seattle in about ten days. My cousin lives here and she wants me to bring all kinds of lei for graduation, you know, for June."

My heart leaps. "I need a lei for commencement. Would you bring me a maile lei like this?"

"Sure. No problem," she smiles. After trading phone numbers, I leave her booth barely able to speak—dumbfounded and delighted that a lei will be arriving fresh for graduation with so little effort. No problem.

The hours quickly evaporate and it is late afternoon already. We must see *Hawai'iloa* before leaving for the Seattle Center. We walk the short distance to the marina where we meet Ray, a tall Hawaiian with long graying hair pulled back into a ponytail. He is giving tours on the canoe. Joan and he discover they are classmates from Kamehameha Schools, a private school exclusively for Hawaiian children in Honolulu. They have not seen each other since graduation, almost thirty years ago. While they "talk-story" and have a mini-reunion, I look around and marvel at the craftsmanship of the many volunteers required to complete this project.

Unlike *Hōkūle'a*, which was constructed with modern materials,

Hawai'iloa was built with the goal of recapturing lost native arts to craft a canoe using only natural materials. The huge steering paddle is koa wood polished to a high gloss, revealing rich golden highlights in the wood. Ray is a member of the Wayfinders of the Pacific, the Washington sponsoring organization for these events. We're chatting casually when he asks, "Hey, would you like to go with us on the canoe back to Lake Union tonight?"

Joan and I look at each other with ever-widening eyes, trying to contain ourselves. Twice in one day, I find myself speechless, but I can feel myself jumping up and down inside. Joan is cool. "Sure, if that's all right." He goes to check with the captain and instructs us to be back at the dock at 6 p.m.

~~~

We are in a traditional Polynesian voyaging canoe being towed from Shilshole Bay into the Ballard Locks en route to Lake Union. While on tour, the canoe does not require a working crew, but many of the crew are in Seattle for the festivities. All on board are Pacific Islanders. All are wearing lei. One of the women is a kumu hula, a teacher of hula, now living in the Seattle area. With her long, curly black hair flowing in the wind, she is blowing the conch shell.

A primal, earthy bass note produces a sound wave of aloha. It's so familiar, and my soul rises. I see and feel the joy emanating from the canoe— an inescapable joy that touches everyone: those on board, those on the shore, those waving from the bridges overhead where traffic has stopped, and those sailing past in other boats.

As I wave to everyone, I am filled with gratitude and aloha. I cannot believe I am here! Such an honor! I marvel at the magic, the convergence of cultures in this piece of water, in this flash of time.

And in me.

This has not been a random series of events. No longer waiting upon the shore, I am moving forward—*i mua!* as Hawaiians would say. The pieces of my life are beginning to fit together. While questions about home seem unresolved, my longing to acknowledge a connection to Hawai'i, my aloha spirit brought me here. Yes, I am *here*, on board this Hawaiian voyaging canoe, eminently capable of traveling thousands of miles in uncharted territory, in calm or turbulent seas. And now the canoe journeys safely and surely in the familiar waters of Seattle's Shilshole Bay, into the Ballard Locks, and docks at the Center for Wooden Boats in Lake Union.

Seattle, a name derived from an indigenous culture. Seattle, a place of home, which has nurtured me, where I have thrived. Seattle, although not an island, is surrounded by the waters of lakes and Puget Sound, reminiscent of another place, a warmer climate, islands in the sun.

The native Hawaiians are here to honor *their* connection to Northwest native tribes, a connection that began in the late 1700s when Hawaiian men became navigators for British trading ships, jumped ship in the Northwest, and married Indian women. This connection persists with the recent gift of giant Sitka spruce logs sent to Hawai'i from the Haida, Tlingit, and Tsimshian tribes of Alaska. A crucial gift. A magnanimous act. These 400-year-old trees, 200 feet tall and eight feet in diameter, were harvested for the hulls of *Hawai'iloa* after the canoe-builders discovered that Hawai'i's native forests no longer produced trees large enough or strong enough for this project.

On this "Voyage of Thanksgiving," *Hōkūle'a* is scheduled to travel south from Seattle along the Pacific Coast to share stories of rediscovery with islanders now living on the West Coast, while *Hawai'iloa* will travel north to British Columbia and Alaska to express appreciation for the generous support by Northwest tribes.

sisters brothers one family
one ocean one sky
ONE
rediscovery cultural renewal healing
celebrate sacred wisdom in all
CANOE
mystical journeying from head to heart
I MUA!

I roamed to find I was most at home where I was born. Seattle is where I reside while Hawai'i is and will forever be Home—where my heart is rooted. The waters of the Pacific Ocean connect these two points and buoy me on my journey of self-discovery.

<div align="center">~~~</div>

I ride this wave of homecoming to the commencement ceremony two weeks later. Standing there on the stage among my professors, university staff and officials, I smell the maile lei around my neck and look out over the audience of 2,000 people. Two thousand! I should not have asked how many people are in the auditorium. I take a deep breath. For a moment, I feel like that five-year-old in a borrowed tutu in kindergarten. But this time, I don't have to figure out what I'm supposed to do. This time I'm not following in anyone's shadow.

I am standing on my own. The work is done. This is my own achievement, my time to be honored—and I honor the many people who supported me in my journey here.

I open my mouth and the words draw us all, those in the room and those not, gently together into a warm current.

~~~

Ancient Hawaiians understood the importance of community. In an ancient canoe chant, everyone chants this stanza. Their voices become one. Everyone in the canoe knows they must work together in order to move forward for the good of all.

I kū wā huki
I kū wā kō
I kū wā a mau
A mau ka ēulu
E huki e
Kūlia!

Together, we pull
Together, we draw (haul)
Together, now and forever
Unceasingly, from the top
Pull (together in full support)
Persevere!

Chapter 20:
Ha'ina

According to the online Hawaiian dictionary *Ulukau*, the meanings for ha'ina are as follows:

> *1. A saying, declaration, statement, explanation; answer, as to a riddle; confession; solution; the two (or sometimes more) last verses of a song that usually begin with the word ha'ina and that repeat the theme of the song, or the name of the person to whom the song is dedicated; to sing the ha'ina of a song; to tell, confess.*

> *2. A breaking, as of a stick or law; a break.*

Ha'ina: to tell, confess, answer a riddle. I needed to find out who I am. This book is my telling. Telling is breaking the silence, breaking the family code: I'm not supposed to tell. Telling is revealing, revealing that we all make mistakes, revealing the secrets that create distance and misunderstanding and a lack of compassion. Telling is also saying what's true for me, regardless if anyone believes or agrees. Telling is breaking through. The words may flow smoothly and slowly like pāhoehoe lava or roughly like bubbling, swift a'ā lava, which hardens with jagged edges that can cut through thin soles and human flesh if someone is careless.

~~~

Love from others has come and gone. Friends, family, lovers. One exception is my mother; I still feel her constant love, her presence. We are yet connected in some way that defies understanding—perhaps a metaphysical umbilical cord. Hawaiians refer to this as piko. Another constant over the decades has been my women friends living here in Seattle and other points near and far. They have taught me about love, both in their relationships with me and with others, including their families, husbands, and lovers.

Learning to love myself has not been self-absorption or self-centeredness. It's about respecting myself, my needs, and my body. It's about having a deep understanding that sharing love requires loving myself first because without self-love, loving others is not possible. I had to learn this: Without loving myself, I have nothing to give.

I've been a slow learner and am still learning. Breaking away from father and family was an act of self-preservation. Marriage was an acceptable escape for a while, but only a rudimentary step toward freedom. Breaking away from my marriage was a leap of faith toward independence and knowing myself, finding my voice.

Self-love generates the strength to refuse to be abused by anyone—family members, friends, bosses, co-workers, lovers. No one has the right to abuse me. Self-love gives me the strength to write and find the words to tell my stories. To tell, not to step on or trash other people. To let go of the hurt and pain, to make things right, to break the cycle of silence that often surrounds abuse, to open a dialogue and give permission for others to tell. Telling reclaims myself, my voice, my power.

Telling also opens the door to compassion. Everyone, I believe, has stories about their families that might sound unbelievable or shocking. I recognize that Dad was not a monster, but there were sides of his personality that terrified us as children. Even his oldest friends might have been shocked to hear about his explosive temper, his lack of patience with his own children, and how he ruled with anger and treated his wife like a child. Although I don't know my father's reasons for establishing his trust, I can conjecture about his motivations: He wanted to ensure that his assets (property and investments) would provide for my mother for the rest of her life and whatever remained would pass down to his children. In other words, he was leaving nothing to chance; because he was nearly twenty years older than Mom, should Mom re-marry, the conditions of the trust protected Dad's estate to ultimately benefit his children. I suppose he recognized he was likely to die first. What he didn't recognize was that Mom had no desire to re-marry; she was happy in her later years, unencumbered by a husband and children. As a consummate autocrat, Dad focused on his own needs. Consequently, he felt no compunction to discuss his estate plans with his wife of forty-plus years, or so I presume. That he provided for her material needs after his death was more than adequate in his mind. While I disagreed with my brother in how he handled the estate, I understand he was obligated to keep the trust open for as long as our mother was alive. If only he had bothered to remind us that this was a condition of the trust. I'm trying to understand these controlling men in my family, but likely will never know the whole truth. Still, there's no excuse for abusive behavior, unkindness, or actions that diminish others.

I'm telling, not because I'm special. I'm telling because I'm *not* special. I'm ordinary; I'm a statistic and my stories of abuse are part of an epidemic that demands outrage. Sexual abuse is sexual abuse no matter what form it takes, and it's far too common. Rape is egregious. Violent or not, remembered or not, rape has long-lasting repercussions on victims. Crimes against children, both girls and boys, when will they stop? I wish I could tell you. Many of these crimes will never be reported, but they are still crimes.

I'm not supposed to tell. But I am. If I tell, maybe my stories will help someone. Maybe these stories will help to make one abuser stop. Maybe one child or adult will take courage and recognize she is not bad and she did nothing wrong.

~~~

I began this memoir to acknowledge the three cultures that have shaped me: Chinese, American, and Hawaiian. Now I can step back and see that my story encompasses a broader perspective. It touches on the many cultures connected by the Pacific Ocean and how they influence each other. These points throughout the Pacific are interlinked and comprise an oceanic community: Peru; the coastal American cities of San Diego, San Francisco, and Seattle; the Canadian city of Vancouver; Alaskan coastal tribes; China; Japan; Okinawa; the Philippines; Vietnam; Aotearoa (New Zealand); Tahiti; the islands of Micronesia and Polynesia; Rapa Nui (Easter Island); and of course, my beloved Hawai'i. And so, while my story is very personal, it also touches on and connects these far-flung points in the Pacific community.

I am complex and multidimensional, with many faces. I am whole and I am fragments. I am past, present, and future. I am predictable and ever-changing.

I am the girl who was raped. I am the daughter who tried to be as good as her brothers—to be seen, recognized, and loved. I am the young woman determined to escape from a family that hoards words. I am the woman who married without knowing who she was or what she really wanted. I am the woman who created a lei of strong women to form a circle around her in friendship to strengthen her heart. I am the woman who became fiercely

170

independent to survive, wielding self-sufficiency as my shield. I am the woman, part-nomadic, determined to live frugally and simply. I am a woman still trying to understand her spirit, to accept all her lessons, mistakes and all, and to come to peace. I am all this and more. Right or wrong, I am my own person.

As I grow in understanding, I know that all these people live within me. I am populated by many, both past and present, maybe even future—all different stages of beingness.

I am full of conflict and contradiction. My family name fights with my individual name for dominance. My impassioned Hawaiian nature is at odds with my passive Chinese-ness. My American outspokenness shocks my Chinese silent tongue.

I'm not supposed to tell. But I am. I have.

I am now strong enough. The years have given me strength to tell my secrets, traumas, and pain: This is what happened, but what happened isn't the entire story. What happened to me defines me yet doesn't define me.

The years come and go. Pain and troubles come and go; they are the layers of lava building up the sides of a mountain. The more lava, the bigger the mountain. A mountain cannot hide itself. It is visible to all those willing to see its beauty.

I am mountain strong. I claim the strength of my ancestors, my mother, my grandmothers from the Lee and Wong clans, and those many unknown and unnamed through past millennia. I honor the strength of my women friends in my various communities. I honor the power of my Holy Trinity: Pele, Kwan Yin, and the dark-skinned Madonna. I honor the beauty in every lava flow.

I am mauna.

I am keiki o ka ʻāina.

~~~

Haʻina ʻia mai,
Ana ka puana.

The dancers sing these words at the end of each hula ʻauana, or modern hula. They mean:

Let my story be told again and again.

171

Acknowledgments

Because many years have lapsed since I first started writing what has become this a book, legions of people have assisted me on this journey: writers and organizations who helped me grow as a writer and develop critical skills. Many dear friends have also accompanied me on this path with their love, encouragement, support. (Yes, attending my readings, especially listening to my early works, definitely count!)

Aloha and Mahalo to the following individuals and organizations,
without whom this book would not have been possible:

Hedgebrook for encouraging and validating women's voices, especially those of marginalized communities; the many women writers whom I've met through Hedgebrook: You have inspired me to continue on this journey, shared insights and information, and demystified the process of getting my work out into the world.

Artist Trust, Jack Straw Cultural Center, and Richard Hugo House for providing programs, workshops, and classes to develop writers to be the best we can be. *The 2014 Jack Straw Writers Anthology* for publishing an excerpt entitled "Being Local."

Willow Books/Aquarius Press, especially publishers Heather Buchanan and Randall Horton, for creating the Willow Books Literature Awards to make dreams come true for underrepresented voices; also Lisa Allen, Antoinette Gardner, and others who gave their talents and support to producing this book.

The Seattle Public Library and King County Library System for offering quiet spaces and invaluable resources.

Lana Abrams at NINE DESIGN for her design expertise on artwork related to my book and the production of publicity materials.

Reginald Dwayne Betts for hearing my voice and getting it, then selecting my manuscript for the 2018 Willow Books Literature Award.

Priscilla Long, whose insightful editing transformed my manuscript into a book I was proud to submit to book contests and various presses. Having the encouragement and support from a writer with decades of experience

172

has been invaluable.

Lilette Subedi for providing a translation for the traditional canoe chant in Chapter 19, offering her expertise on local and Hawaiian culture, as well as the Hawaiian language, and remembering my father's Chinatown store.

Members of my writing groups of recent years as I completed, polished, and revised my manuscript: Janice Knight Cook, Aura Cuevas, Esther Altshul Helfgott, Trish McKenney Honig, Ann B. Hursey, Connie Lee Tuttle.

Early readers of my manuscript: Liz Aulsebrook, Laura Cooper, Ann Hedreen, Nina Krebs, Stella Mortenson, Nan Macy, Marge Herman Osborne.

My friends in Seattle and Honolulu who have witnessed, supported, and encouraged me. Your compassion and friendship have bolstered me to keep going even when I wasn't sure what I was doing.

The many teachers who pushed me to work harder, think more deeply, and move beyond my comfort zone, especially at Port Townsend Writers Conference, VONA (Voices of our Nations Arts), Oxford Nonfiction Writers Conference, and Las Dos Brujas Writers Workshop. Denise Chavez gave me the mantra: "I am mountain strong!" Faith Adiele encouraged me to report from the body, to let the body speak.

The various Hawaiian cultural organizations, especially in the Pacific Northwest, working to keep alive Hawaiian music and cultural values for islanders, often far-flung, and reminding us of our connection to our beloved islands.

The University of Washington, Bothell, whose demanding academic writing requirements, while daunting, reawakened my desire to produce creative writing.

These books were invaluable to me: *Volcanoes of the National Parks in Hawai'i* by Gordon A. McDonald and Douglass H. Hubbard; *Pele: Goddess of Hawai'i's Volcanoes* by Herb Kawainui Kane.

About the Author

Loreen Lilyn Lee is a Chinese American writer born in Honolulu, T.H. (Territory of Hawai'i). Issues of identity intrigue her, and her fiction and nonfiction often reflect multiple cultures and cultural intersections. She has received fellowships from Hedgebrook and the Jack Straw Writers Program. She lives in Seattle, Washington, where she also tutors English and writing.